Clear	Position	Sum	Cipher group
M	12	4+8	GREEN BL...
E	5	5	BLUE
E	5	2+3	ORANGE RED
T	19	5+6+8	BLUE VIOLET BROWN
M	12	3+4+5	RED GREEN BLUE
E	5	1+4	YELLOW GREEN
T	19	4+7+8	GREEN OLIVE BROWN
H	8	2+6	ORANGE VIOLET
I	9	4+5	GREEN BLUE
S	18	5+6+7	BLUE VIOLET OLIVE
E	5	1+2+2	YELLOW ORANGE ORANGE
V	20	5+7+8	BLUE OLIVE BROWN
E	5	1+1+3	YELLOW YELLOW RED
N	13	6+7	VIOLET OLIVE
I	9	3+6	RED VIOLET
N	13	5+8	BLUE BROWN
G	7	3+4	RED GREEN

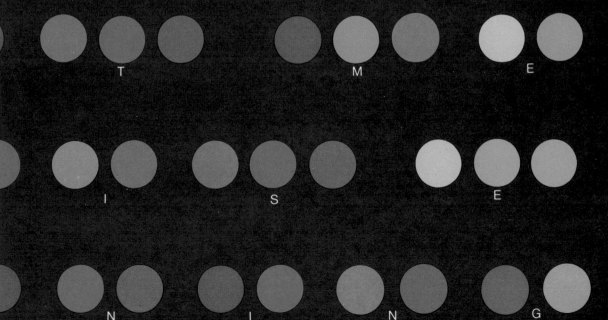

T   M   E

I   S   E

N   I   N   G

First published in Great Britain in 1976 by
JUPITER BOOKS (LONDON) LIMITED 167 Hermitage Road, London N4
ISBN 0 904041 41 7

Copyright © 1976 Holt, Rinehart and Winston
Printed in Hong Kong

Secret language

Secret language

Communicating in Codes and Ciphers

Julian A. Bielewicz

JUPITER BOOKS 1976

Acknowledgements

Amalgamated Wireless Australia, pp. 62, 64, 66.
Australian Broadcasting Commission, p. 63.
Biblioteque Nationale, Paris, pp. 10, 109.
British Museum, pp. 5, 16, 42, 45.
Department of Physics, University of Sydney, p. 75.
Gregory, R., pp. 2, 6, 7, 12, 14, 27, 32, 33, 34-35, 38, 42, 43,
44, 45, 46, 49, 51, 58, 60, 61, 84, and back endpaper.
Kahn, David, *The Codebreakers*, Weidenfeld and
Nicolson, 1966, for text of Pannizardi telegram, p.10;
Adams despatch, p.16; and Wheatstone's description of
the Playfair cipher, p.45.
Koch, *The Book of Signs*, Dover, pp. 52, 83.
Louvre Museum, p. 4.
Postmaster General's Department, OTC Branch, pp. 56,
57, 61, 71, 73, 74.
Public Records Office, London, p. 9.
Publishing Art, pp. 1, 2, 3, 8, 15, 20, 21, 23, 25, 26, 48, 49,
54, 59, 69, 76, 77, 78, 79, 80, 82, 83, 85, 86, endpapers and
cover.
US National Archives, pp. 16, 17, 19, 47.

Contents

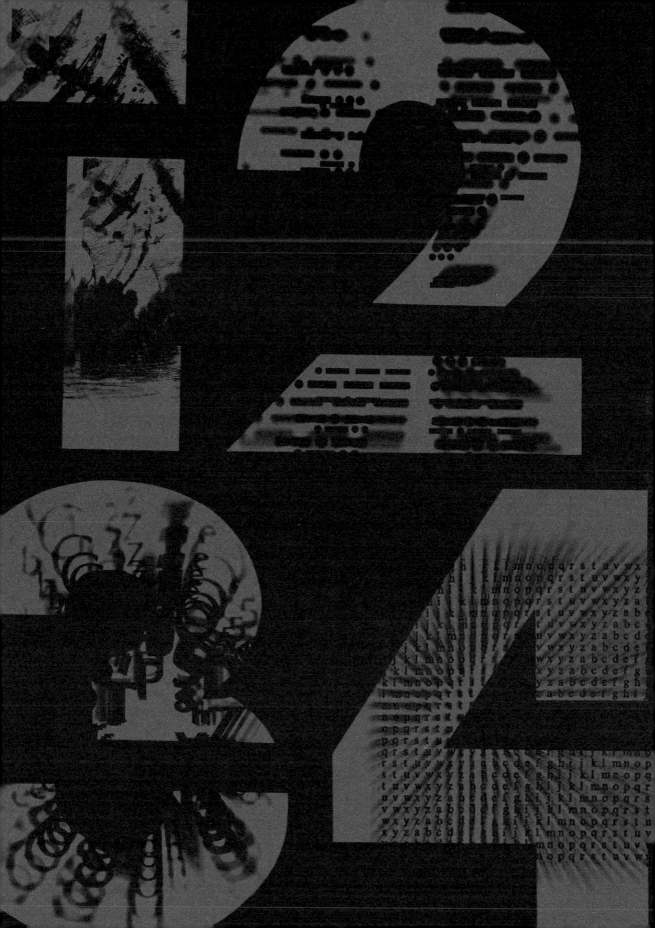

Introduction

Gordon Lonsdale, master-spy for Russia in the West. Arrested in Britain and sentenced to twenty-five years imprisonment, Lonsdale was exchanged for Britisher Greville Wynne in 1964.

Mystery, intrigue and danger surround the activities of concealment and discovery of the closely guarded secrets of nations and powerful organisations. This is the shadowy world of espionage whose heroes in fiction have thrilled us for generations, but whose figures in the real world of security scandals and trials often seem remote.

The main work of the secret agent in peace or war, in military, diplomatic or industrial espionage, is to discover the secrets of others. Sometimes he must also reveal information, worthless and misleading, but also highly secret. In every case, suitable means of passing on the information he is dealing with — or she is dealing with, for some of the most famous practitioners of the art of spying have been women — is essential to the work. In struggles between countries intelligence plays a vital role, but a great deal of the value of uncovering the secrets of opponents lies in allowing them to believe that their secrets are still secure. For if such messages fall into the hands of the rightful owners of the information they must know that their secret has leaked and can at the very least take measures to minimise the effect of the leakage, if not to capture the agent.

Thus no open means of communication can serve between the agent and his fellows or his headquarters. Secret ways of passing on information are essential. From earliest times, therefore, men have devised ways of communicating in secret and of hiding the true meaning of their secret messages. The science of *cryptology* and the invention of codes and ciphers have arisen out of this need. Through the ages, ways of physically concealing the messages themselves have been developed. These have ranged from writing on the shaven heads of slaves — whose hair had then to be let grow to hide the message and shaved again to read it — to modern high-speed radio transmission in code.

1 *Picture writing recording the passing of a party of soldiers and surveyors. Both North American Indians and the Mayas used symbols like these.*

2 *Message sticks of the Australian Aboriginals. The messengers who carried them delivered messages orally. Not true writing, the carvings on the sticks were symbols that guaranteed that the messenger was telling the truth.*

Codes and ciphers are only slightly different ways of concealing the *meaning* of messages, and secret means of transmission are often necessary for both. This book deals with all three of these aspects of secret communication, but its main purpose is to give a brief introduction to some of the ways of concealing the true meanings of secret messages and some of the methods that are used to discover them when such messages are received or intercepted. This is the science of *cryptology*.

It is impossible to say definitely when cryptology was born, but it must have its beginnings in the time when men first needed to use the gift of language to hide their true feelings of belligerence or fear from their fellows. The earliest confirmed examples of the use of a secret language seem to be among the ancient Egyptians, who are known to have used at least three hieroglyphic ciphers, as was discovered in 1932 by the French archaeologist, Jean Francois Champollian. It is not definitely known, however, whether these were really intended to hide meanings or merely to mystify the casual reader.

The birth of cryptology as we know it came with the need to transmit messages which the sender could not afford to have known to the enemy. The smoke signals of the American Indians mystified the frontiersmen of the American west just as the drum beats of African tribesmen puzzled the first intruders into their regions. These signals, like the message sticks of the Australian Aboriginals, are all primitive codes. As civilisation advanced, the ways of sending secret messages became more complex, for men began to invent ways to discover their true meanings.

Although it was possible for a Greek nobleman in ancient Persia to use a very simple method to warn the Greeks that

Extract from Jean Francois Champollian's account of his decipherment of the famous Rosetta Stone.

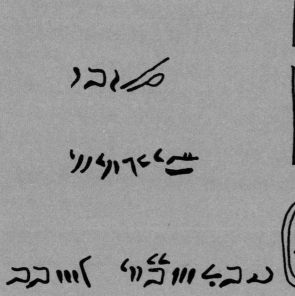

Ancient secret writing. A cuneiform tablet from Uruk bearing a bi-lingual text in honour of the goddess Ishtar.

Egyptian hieroglyphs.

the Persians were preparing an attack, the Romans already were using actual *secret writing*. In Persia, Demaratus the Greek wrote his message 'in clear' on a wooden tablet from which the usual wax writing surface had been scraped. The wax was then reapplied and the messengers carrying the blank tablet were allowed by Persian guards to cross the frontier. The Spartan leaders received and read the message and the famous battle of Thermopylae was one of the results. This, of course, was *hidden*, not secret writing. But Julius Caesar himself records the use of a simple code — which he wrote in Greek characters — and this was true secret writing or *cryptography*.

Aeneas Tacticus, a Greek writing some four centuries before Christ, in one of the earliest books on the conduct of war, included one of the first treatises on cryptography, and many Greek codes and ciphers have survived until today. Although it is known that cryptography was not uncommon in Roman times — other leading Romans besides Caesar are known to have used it — most of the Roman books about it have been lost.

The Arabs, who took over so much of Greek and Roman science, developed much of the basis of modern mathematics and had great skill both in cryptography and the 'breaking' of codes and ciphers. The word 'cipher' comes from Arabic, and the Arabs are indeed the first cryptologists in the modern sense. Their messengers in contact with European and Eastern rulers in the great days of the Arab Empire had much use for secret writing and just as great a need to understand the secret writings of others. There were great Arabian cryptologists like Mausili and Qalqashandi in the early fourteenth century and later. To us it might seem that the Arab language

alone would be secret enough, but from earliest times the great rulers have employed skilled interpreters, and these men were often cryptologists as well.

But it was the world of diplomacy and warfare of the early European states that developed the modern science. This was especially true in Italy, where scholars re-translated ancient Greek and Roman works from the Arabic translations which by then were often the only copies known to exist. No doubt in this way the men of the Renaissance learnt from Greek, Roman and Arab works on cryptology and then further developed it. The Popes and the rulers of Venice, Florence and Milan had great need to send and discover secret messages and could only conduct their complicated negotiations by such means. So important did the science become that Gabriel di Lavinde of Parma, a secretary of the Antipope Clement VII of Avignon — wrote a detailed study of it in 1379.

As modern states developed in the rest of Europe and diplomatic intrigue and warfare became almost universal, the use and importance of cryptography spread. The French, British and Spanish were compelled to hide the contents of their diplomatic correspondence and the reports of their generals from each other and from other nations as well. Cryptology in Britain, for example, was greatly developed by the first Queeen Elizabeth's minister, Sir Francis Walsingham, who used and trained spies and cryptographers to uncover the plots of Philip of Spain and Mary Queen of Scots. The skill of Walsingham's agents resulted in the conviction and execution of Mary on the charge of treason — actually a plot to assassinate Elizabeth.

Sir Francis Walsingham, spymaster of Elizabeth I.

Walsingham's agent, Thomas Phelippes, forged this postscript to Mary's enciphered letter. This led to the discovery of the conspirators to the plot to assassinate Elizabeth.

The postscript reads: I would be glad to know the names and qualities of the six gentlemen which are to accomplish the designment; for that it may be I shall be able, upon knowledge of the parties, to give you some further advice necessary to be followed therein. . . . As also from time to time, particularly how you proceed: and as soon as you may, for the same purpose, who be already, and how far every one, privy unto.

The tragic Mary Queen of Scots. Convicted of treason, she was executed.

55

HER MAJESTY'S STATE PAPER OFFICE

May 1586 June

Incorrect
If Captain Dreyfus has not had relations with you, it would be wise to have the ambassador deny it officially. Our emissary is warned.

Correct
If Captain Dreyfus has not had relations with you, it would be wise to have the ambassador deny it officially, to avoid press comment.

The two decipherments of the Pannizardi telegram. Note the different versions of the last four words

The famous Pannizardi telegram enciphered in an adapted commercial code, the Italian Baravelli code. In 1894, French Army Captain Alfred Dreyfus was arrested on suspicion of espionage. In this most famous of espionage trials, Dreyfus was convicted, largely on the basis of an early and inaccurate decipherment of this message. It was sent to Rome by the Italian military attache in Paris, Colonel Alessandro Pannizardi.
All diplomatic telegrams were copied for and decoded by the Foreign Ministry at that time. The first decipherment of the message implied that Dreyfus had spied for Italy. Later, the correctly deciphered message was suppressed. It took till 1906 completely to clear Dreyfus, by which time the real culprit was known.

During the eighteenth and nineteenth centuries cryptology became an almost universal practice, and non-secret codes came into existence for the use of merchants, bankers and businessmen as the use of morse telegraphy became vital to expanding business as well as diplomatic operations.

Codes and ciphers are methods of writing messages in such a way that only those who possess the *key* can make sense of them. The message is either *encoded* or *enciphered*, and sometimes both — the encoded message can be sent in cipher. The end result is the *cryptogram*. When it is received or intercepted the cryptogram is *decoded* or *deciphered* to find its hidden meaning. The art of writing such messages is known as *cryptography;* the study of ways to write and decipher them is *cryptology*, both words coming from Greek words meaning 'secret', or 'hidden'; 'writing'; and 'the science or study of'.

When secret messages are captured or fall accidentally into the wrong hands, the enemy must set out to solve or 'break' the code or cipher, no easy task without the key. The art of breaking codes and ciphers is *cryptanalysis*. Cryptography and cryptanalysis together form the science of cryptology.

In this book we look first at cryptography — the art of putting messages into code or cipher. The second part deals with cryptanalysis or *codebreaking*, and then goes on to look briefly at some of the more complex aspects of cryptology. Throughout, and at the end in a special section, there are cryptograms for you to try your new skill.

The language of code breakers

Anagram   A word or phrase whose letters can be rearranged to form another word of phrase. For example, ON is the anagram of NO.

Biliteral   Using or consisting of two letters.

Cipher   A method of secret writing that replaces each character or figure of the original with a different letter or symbol, or achieves the same effect by disarranging the original order of the letters.

Clear   *see* Plaintext

Code   A system which substitutes certain symbols, words, or groups of letters for the words or phrases or whole messages of plaintext.

Cryptanalysis   The technique of deciphering or decoding secret messages without access to the code or key.

Cryptogram   The secret message in code or cipher.

Cryptography   The study of secret communications.

Decipher / Decode To take a secret message and convert it into plaintext by the use of a key or a cipher.

Encipher / Encode To put a plaintext message into cipher or code.

Frequency table   A list of letters, or groups of letters, digraphs, trigraphs, etc. in the order of frequency of their occurrence in normal plaintext.

Grille   A card with apertures through which the words or letters of the secret message can be written, leaving spaces to be completed with a covering text.

Keyword   A word used to set the pattern of a code or cipher in such a way that the message cannot be deciphered without obtaining or discovering it.

Key   The book or list of plain equivalents to codewords.

Nulls   Extra meaningless letters inserted in or added to a coded or enciphered message to complete the letter groups or patterns, or to hide word breaks.

Palindrome   A word or phrase that reads the same backwards as forwards, e.g., Eve.

Plaintext (*or* Clear) The original message in ordinary language.

Most people, at one time or another, have probably sent some friend a secret message. One of the oldest means of doing this, and still a very common one, is invisible ink. The Arabs used it, as did German agents in World War II. So, for all its simplicity, it opens the gates to the strange and fascinating world of secret communication. For the expense of a little small change at the greengrocer's, anyone can try this adventure.

Squeeze the juice of a lemon into a dish. Write your message with a toothpick or some other similar instrument, being careful not to press the point into the surface. Vital messages have been betrayed by this. While still wet the message remains visible, but when the juice dries the words disappear. Heat the paper, and the message reappears. A 150-watt light bulb is sufficient. After the paper has been held close to the bulb for a few moments the writing begins to show up.

A little more mystery surrounds the use of invisible ink which does not have to be heated to be read. A quarter-teaspoon of iron-sulphate (from your chemist) is mixed with a quarter-cup of tap-water. Again, use a toothpick or something similar to write with.

To read the invisible writing one has to know another secret formula. A quarter-teaspoon of washing soda is mixed with a quarter-cup of water. Washing soda is not always so easily found today, but a good old-fashioned grocer will be able to help. Mix the solution, dab it on the letter with cottonwool and the message will slowly begin to reveal itself.

CAUTION: As chemicals are often dangerous in that they can poison or cause painful burns, keep them out of the reach of young children.

Invisible inks have their disadvantages. First, they remain invisible for only a few days before beginning to show up of their own accord (lemon juice lasts a little longer than iron sulphate). So speedy delivery is essential. Second, if the message falls into the wrong hands, a blank page is an almost certain giveaway that invisible ink has been used. Any serious user therefore usually writes the secret message between the lines. After all, a basic concept of secret communication is to use one message to conceal another.

A safe method is needed for delivering the secret message. Even in the two great world wars, despite strict censorship, regular postal and cable services carried innumerable secret messages. So, for our innocent letter with its invisible message, probably the post office is the simplest answer. In its sealed envelope your message does have added secrecy. Only the person to whom it is addressed will see its contents. True, envelopes can be steamed open, but in our case this seems unlikely. Although in Vienna in the eighteenth century the famous Black Chamber — a special group of government-paid cryptanalysts — did open, examine and reseal *all* diplomatic mails in and out of the city, our regular mails are unlikely to be so closely watched today!

An alternative is to deliver the message personally, or entrust it to some friend. In the days before recognised postal and telegraphic services, trusted friends and messengers were the only ways to deliver messages safely. Walsingham used hundreds of them all over Europe. The obvious disadvantage is that the messenger may be intercepted, or even bribed. During the American War of Independence the couriers of both sides were often caught, and there are thrilling tales of some of their exploits.

Secret writing in lemon juice
Squeeze a lemon into a cup or egg cup.

With a toothpick, write out your message "between the lines".

To read the message, heat the paper at a 150-watt globe.

In chemical ink:
Mix a quarter-teaspoon of iron-sulphate with a quarter-cup of water.

Write the message as before.

Mix a quarter-teaspoon of washing soda with a quarter-cup of water.

Dab on message with cotton wool and wait for message to reveal itself.

Dear John,
Glad to hear that you are well on the way to recovery. It can't be much fun having your tonsils out!

Meet me at the hide-out tomorrow 7 o'clock. Urgent news to discuss. Pass this message on to David.

I hope to visit you next week.

Yours,
Harry

2

copy

I have heard

was against a d
5. 18. 100   72. 56. 81. 74. 62. 68. 92.   22.   54

thinking   that
67. 21. 92.

war   were   not
69. 22. 12.   5. 2. 52. 98.

men

1 *George Washington. Couriers brought him agents' reports of British troop movements in the American War of Independence.*

2 *John Quincey Adams, American Minister to Berlin. The British Black Chamber read despatches between him and his colleagues in London and the Hague between 1798 and 1800.*

Despatch to John Quincy Adams, American Minister in Berlin in 1789, deciphered by the Decyphering Branch — the British Government's Black Chamber

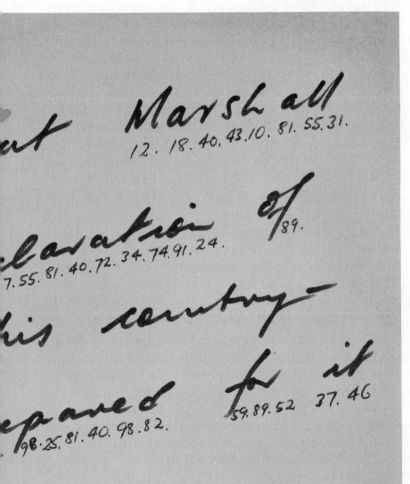

Modern agents often use a *drop*. A *drop* can be almost
anything anywhere – a litter-bin in some public park or a
tree with a convenient hole. The message is left at the drop
on a given day at a given time by one agent and is collected
by another. There are great dangers also in the drop. It can
only work securely if both agents are in close proximity to
each other, preferably with the collecting agent nearby to
keep an eye on proceedings. As secret agents are very often
under suspicious observation, this has often led to
discovery. Also the *dropped* message might even be picked
up by accident and thus fail to reach its destination.

In real-life espionage secret messages usually have to be
sent from one country to another by the fastest possible
means, particularly in times of war, when a day's delay
could mean the difference between victory and defeat.
Reliable as the postal services are, they lack the speed
which is so often a vital factor when important
information has to be passed on. This usually calls for the
use of a telephone, radio transmitter, telegram or cable.

In both World Wars there are famous instances of the use
of international cables, or telegrams — and the regular
postal services — to pass on critical secret information.
One of the most fascinating of these is the so-called
Zimmermann telegram. Late in 1916, Britain was
desperately anxious to bring the United States into the
war, and Germany was anxious to avoid this. Arthur
Zimmermann, the German Foreign Minister, sent by
international cable a famous telegram in code to his
Washington and Mexico City ambassadors. This
telegram proposed that Mexico should declare war on the
United States, so that, fighting in Mexico, she would be
unable to send troops to France. The British Admiralty's
famous Room 40 (like the Viennese Black Chamber)

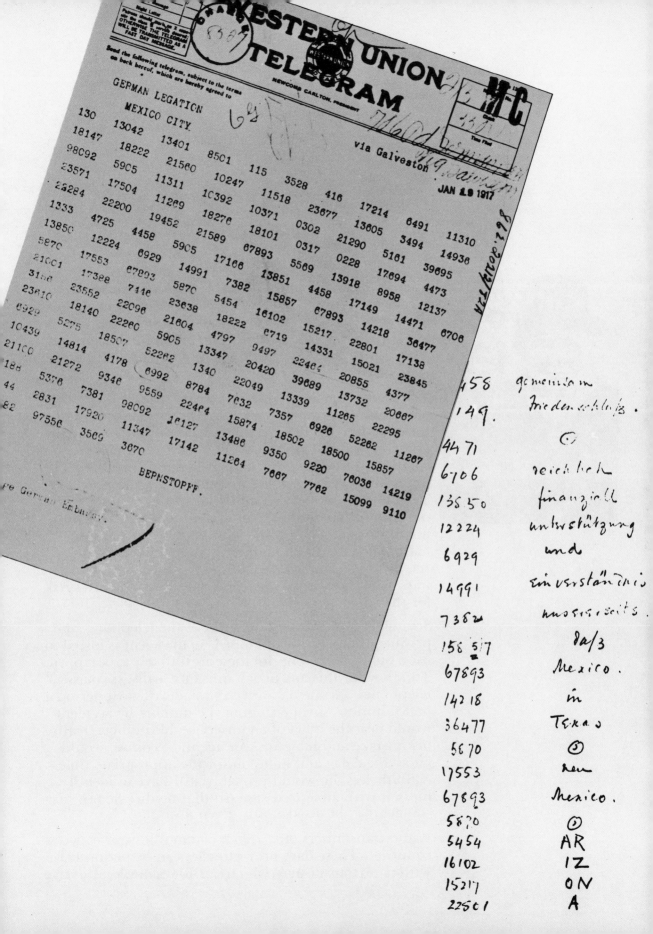

intercepted and decoded the cable, and made it known to President Wilson. In the cable, Zimmermann made it clear that Germany was about to use submarines to sink any ship in the North Atlantic, including American ones. The United States declared war and Britain and France were saved.

Telephones are readily available and overseas telephoning is improving every year, especially with the introduction of STD, although delays still occur and the assistance of the operator is often needed. An agent wanting to telephone his masters in another country will not wish to give away the number he is calling. Telephones do offer fast and relatively secret communication within a country, but they can be *tapped*, not always only by people whose job it is to protect national security. Though spymasters use electronic *scrambler* devices which make eavesdropping almost impossible, the use of the telephone always involves risk for the agent.

Scramblers work from both ends of the telephone, and private phones are often tapped, so the agent is forced to use a public telephone, for these are unlikely to be tapped. To allow for this and avoid 'nuisance' calls, spymasters' telephones operate on a given time delay, say one and a half minutes. Anyone ringing the number by accident would hear the howl of an unserviceable number, realise his mistake and hang up. An agent, of course, would know the delay and hang on for the appropriate time. Nevertheless, he would probably still have to identify himself with an agreed sign, so that neither he nor his contact may be accidentally given away.

Radio transmitters offer quick communication between countries. These days near miracles can be performed with radio transmitters, which can, for example, also have

scramblers fitted to them. Telephones can also be attached to transmitters. Then there is high-speed radio transmission, which enables the agent to transmit several hundred words per minute. Tape recorders with variable speeds are used to receive such messages at high speed, and then to replay them at an understandable sixty words or so per minute.

Radio transmissions can be detected, even if the nature of the message remains unknown, and the more regular or frequent the transmissions, the easier it becomes to pinpoint the area from which they are being sent. A great danger here is that the enemy may take over the transmitter, replace the agent with one of his own men and feed out incorrect information, though this is usually safeguarded against by the use of an agreed code word to open transmissions, or an agreed signal that the transmitter has been captured. In wartime or tense conditions between nations, a close watch is kept on unauthorised radio transmissions. Special vans with rotating aerials are used to patrol the areas where such transmissions are expected. As the aerial rotates, the direction of the strongest signal is established, and the vans converge on the transmitter. In World War II, British Intelligence's radio with the Dutch underground was located in this way. Very cleverly, the responsible German counter-intelligence officer did not reveal the capture of the agent, who was compelled to transmit false information. When the agent, Hubertus Lauwers, at great risk to himself succeeded in including in a false transmission the agreed sign to indicate such a takeover, London headquarters refused to believe the network had been broken. As a result, over a hundred agents lost their lives. Modern transmitters can depend on the tonal quality of the agent's voice, but, of course, voice transmission is not always used. When it is, the enemy would need experts on voice production and have tapes of the agent's voice before deceiving his masters at the other end. The slightest alteration would set off a whole series of warning alarms. But the greatest danger is the capture of the agent and his interrogation with the use of modern electronic tortures and drugs. Few men can withstand such interrogation for long.

Telegrams are hardly private. The message has to be seen by at least two other men. It would therefore be quite ridiculous for any agent to send a message without some attempt to disguise the meaning of the words. Zimmermann sent one of his two famous telegrams in a very difficult code. Unfortunately for him, he sent a second one which gave a clue to the first, and was easier to decipher. Once a message has betrayed the agent he can be fed with false information such as Lauwers was forced to transmit and all sorts of complications arise. But no matter what method is used to transmit information, added security comes from first encoding or enciphering the message.

Codes, ciphers and secret transmissions are by no means modern inventions. The Spartans who read Demaratus' message were for many years at war with Athens. To send each other information they used a very simple but effective method. A belt was wound round a stick (called a *scytale*) and the message was written on the belt along the length of the stick. The belt was then unwound and worn or otherwise delivered to its destination. The message was read by winding the belt around a stick exactly the same size as the one used when it was written.

You can easily make a similar device. Use a number of pencils, depending on how many need to be in on the secret. Make sure all the pencils are the same size and thickness. Now take a strip of paper, about a centimetre wide and twenty-five or thirty centimetres long. Secure one end of the strip to the pencil and write the message along the length of the pencil. When you reach the end of the pencil turn it around a little and start a new line. When you unwind the strip, it will look something like the drawing.

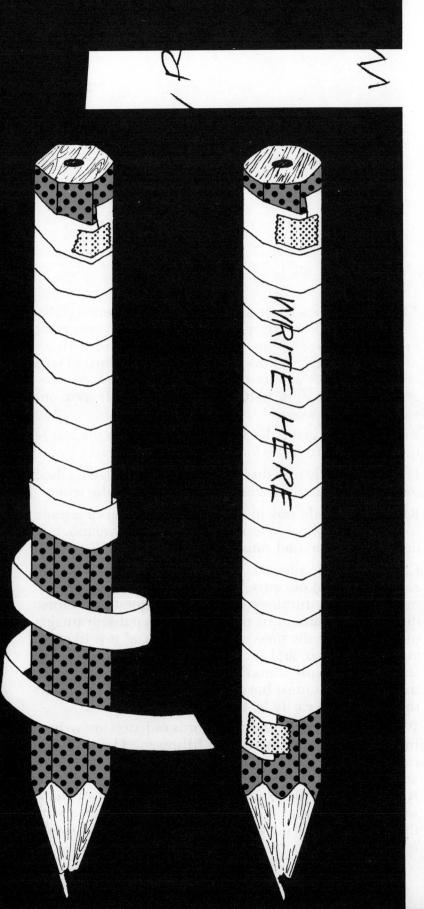

The Spartan scytale.

To make its modern equivalent, take several large pencils. A six-sided 'giant' is ideal. Give them to your correspondents.

Take a paper strip about a centimetre wide and thirty centimetres long and wind it around the pencil in a spiral, so that the edges touch.

Fasten the ends with tape.

Write a line of the message on each face of the pencil.

Unwrap the completed message and send it to the holders of the other pencils.

The famous French statesman, Cardinal Richelieu (1585-1642), used another ingenious simple system. This is the *grille*, which was no more than a sheet of card with a number of holes cut into it. Whenever he wanted to send one of his many agents a secret message, he placed the grille over a sheet of writing paper. Each hole took one word of the message.

Removing the grille, Richelieu then filled in the rest of the sheet to give it the look of an innocent letter.

His agents easily read the hidden message by placing their own grilles, identical with Richelieu's, over the letter.

Richelieu's grille was in fact a simplification of a more sophisticated one developed by Girolamo Cardano, a doctor of Milan, and published by him in 1556.

Cardano's grille allowed single letters only to be placed in each space, and of course the task of completing the message in a natural-seeming way is a good deal more difficult. Of course, this is one of the great disadvantages of the grille. If the message seems artificial it is likely to attract suspicion, and the whole idea is that the message should seem quite innocent. The other disadvantage is that each agent must have his own grille, and the grilles themselves can easily be lost or stolen.

When using a grille, the code words or letters are written in first, then comes the task of filling in. The filling-in must fit in with the key words of letters, otherwise they will be recognisable at once. In a short message with the Richilieu grille this is easy enough, but if there are many words filling in may not prove so simple. Of course, with the Cardano grille it is a matter of using a *word* to hide the *letter*.

report

to

at

me

Once

My dear friend,

I heard a report that it is likely to rain heavily for at least the next week. Dear me if this goes on at the present rate we will all drown. Once it starts it seems to pour for ever.

Making a grille like Richelieu's is quite simple.

Take a sheet of cardboard the same size as the writing pad you intend to use. You will need to keep the same size for convenience in all messages for which the grille is used.

Cut half a dozen to a dozen holes, depending on the size decided upon, and arranged to fit along the lines. When the first grille has been prepared in this way, use it as a stencil to cut out the others.

When using a grille, the secret words or letters are written in first, then comes the task of filling in. The filling-in must fit in with the secret words or letters, otherwise they will be recognisable at once. In a short message with the Richilieu grille this is easy enough, but if there are many words filling-in may not prove so simple. Of course, with the Cardano grille it is a matter of using a word to hide the letter.

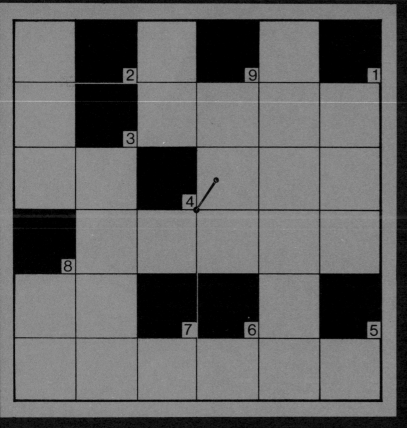

The modern development of Cardano's grille is more complicated and more effective. The German Army used it in World War I.

Make a grid of 36 squares each say, 1 cm square. Plot nine squares, as described in the note below and number them.

To test the grille, place it on a sheet of notepaper, and take the message

**SUFFERED
CASUALTIES
NEED
REINFORCEMENTS**

Write the first nine letters of the message in order in the holes—say counter clockwise.

Rotate the grille a quarter turn and write out the next nine letters.

Continue till message is complete. If the message does not need thirty-six letters, complete with nulls. For nulls, repeat some of the letters you have used already, in meaningless order, to confuse the enemy.

Transcribe into six-letter groups on a fresh page

To decipher, rearrange letters in six groups of six, place grille over message and repeat procedure above, writing down letters.

Note. Make sure that no hole in the grille falls twice in the same position. To do this, draw the grille first on tracing paper, with a copy. Put a pin through the centre. Plot the holes and turn the grille to each position. Then cut it out of card.

Sir Francis Bacon invented his own secret cipher.

Sir Francis Bacon (1561-1626), Lord Chancellor of England, recognised as a philosopher and man-of-letters, devised a code system which depended on marking characters in an innocent-looking letter. The letter was written first and coded afterwards, but first Bacon invented his own special *cipher*, using only the letters *a* and *b*.

Francis Bacon's cipher

A	aaaaa	I-J	abaaa	R	baaaa
B	aaaab	K	abaab	S	baaab
C	aaaba	L	ababa	T	baaba
D	aaabb	M	ababb	U-V	baabb
E	aabaa	N	abbaa	W	babaa
F	aabab	O	abbab	X	babab
G	aabba	P	abbba	Y	babba
H	aabbb	Q	abbbb	Z	babbb

Bacon would then write his innocent note, such as

Glad to hear that you are recovering from your recent illness. I am well myself.

27

and certain letters would be marked, either by writing them in a heavier hand, using a dot, or lightly underlining them. All the marked letters represent B, the unmarked letters A.

Glad to hear that you are recovering from your recent illness. I am well myself.

The receiver rearranged the innocent message into its groups of five letters and used the cipher to read off the real meaning.

Gladt ohear youar ereco verin gfrom yourr ecent

baaaa aabaa abbba abbab baaaa baaba aaaaa baaba

R E P O R T A T

illne sslam wellm yself

abbab abbaa aaaba aabaa

O N C E

Methods like Bacon's were used quite recently. In nineteenth-century England, letters were expensive to send, but newspapers travelled cheaply. Poor people were able to send messages by marking letters in old newspapers with small dots, and sending these cheaply. Bacon's cipher contained the beginnings of another cipher practice that is now very widely used. That is the sending of the message in groups which hide the original arrangement of letters in the message and thus make the cipher more difficult to break.

It is not absolutely necessary to use letters or notes with Bacon's code. Messages can be delivered using a pack of cards. All the red cards might represent A, the black ones B. The pack is sent after the cards have been arranged in a certain order. Take the word REPORT for example. The arrangement of the cards would go something as follows: a red card followed by four black ones (*baaaa* = R); two black, a red and two more black cards (*abbba* = P) and so on till the message is complete.

Again, a simple box of chocolates could be used. A mixture of plain and milk chocolates would serve the purpose. The darker ones could represent *a*, the lighter ones, *b*.Starting from the top left-hand corner, the chocolates are arranged according to Bacone's cipher.

Books have often been used as cipher keys. The sender and the receiver need copies of the same book, for example the popular *Treasure Island*. One particular page might be marked in the way described above, or one could underline whole key words on a given page. Take the message

TIME TO EXPLORE THE PLAN

Now find it in this passage from *Biggles Flies South* by W.E. Johns (page 120)

"We shall have plenty of time to explore it.
I can see lots of dates, so let's get a
good supply and start back. Another point
is, the side of the hill we came down is still
in the shade; when the sun gets round a bit
later on, it will be nearly too hot to touch."
"Yes, I think that's the best plan,"
agreed Ginger.

If the appropriate words were underlined, the message would at once be clear.

Of course this is a very simple example. More complex information can be passed using this basic idea, although it is by no means always so convenient to find the correct words. A simpler idea is to underline individual letters. Using the same passage we can send the message

NEED HELP

We shall have plen*t*y of tim*e* to *e*xplore it.
I can see lots of *d*ates, so let's get a good
supply and start back. Anot*he*r point is,
the side of the hi*l*l we came down is still
in the shade; when the sun gets round a bit,
later on, it will be nearly too hot to touch."
"Yes, I think that's the best *p*lan," agreed
Ginger.

Anyone who saw the first television series of *Colditz*, shown in both Australia and Britain, cannot fail to have been impressed by the way in which one American prisoner (played by filmstar Robert Wagner) attempted to get information through the German censors to the

United States. To write a book aimed to convince Americans not to enter the war, while a captive, is a mammoth undertaking in itself, but to arrange Chapter Four so that every ninth letter is part of a coded message is a staggering task. In the same series a British prisoner (played by David McCallum of UNCLE fame), set up an elementary code with his wife. When she wrote of blackouts, this told the prisoner that parts of his last letter had been censored.

The code involving the ninth letter is extremely difficult to execute, but remains effective. Shorter messages are easier to arrange. Take the innocent note

Everyone hopes that Eddie and Alice are popular.

On the surface, it could refer perhaps to a showbiz duo, but if we take out every ninth letter, we have

Everyone *h*opes that *E*ddie and A*l*ice are po*p*ular

H   E   L   P

It is, of course, not mandatory to use every ninth letter; every fourth, sixth, or any other regularly occuring letter would be equally effective.

With the exception of Bacon's cipher, the various ideas we have so far explored are not, strictly speaking, codes or ciphers. They are strictly *concealment methods*.

In codes, words, phrases and even whole sentences are replaced by a code word or phrase. On a simple level, the message

THE SKY IS OVERCAST

might refer to a bombing mission, whereas the message

THE SKY IS EXPECTED TO CLEAR

may refer to the cancellation of some bombing mission. It is easy to invent an infinite number of phrases of this nature.

A slightly more complicated system involves the replacement of *key words* with *code words*. Key words might be enemy, attack, weapons. Now take the *code* word

RAMON

RAMON SEEMS ACTIVE

could refer to the enemy's forces moving to some position.

It is easy to vary the form of the code word, and

RAMIN IS DELAYED

might refer to the enemy's naval force, and RAMEN could be the variation for the enemy's air force. There is an infinite variety of possible code words and code variations which can be employed. Of course, simple variations like these are extremely easy for an enemy to work out if a message is intercepted.

In the message

ALBERT LEFT FOR LONDON ON TUESDAY

the idea is similar. Here ALBERT could be the code word for the enemy's fleet; LONDON the code for some other port; while TUESDAY could refer to the number of troops being carried or even to Tuesday itself, if this is not giving too much away, for the enemy would surely know on which day its fleet left.

There is an infinite variety of possible code words and their variations, so no-one can be expected to memorise every one. To overcome this difficulty, *code books* are used. They are indispensible. tools for agents employing codes. Code books contain all the variations that the agent needs to know in order to communicate with his headquarters or with fellow agents.

Like every *concealment method*, code books have their good and bad points. Their biggest advantages are that codes are easy to use but very difficult to break. Most navies, including the British and German, use codes contained in substantial books.

Imagine that an agent intercepts the message

ALBERT EXPECTED TO RETURN SUNDAY

and suspects it to be a code, where does he start? Without some inside information, like knowing what the message *might* be referring to, his task is almost impossible. Given sufficient intercepted messages, counter-intelligence in time begins to suspect the nature of the assignment and from there can go on to begin to crack the essentials of any code in use. All take time, and in most situations time is against the counter-intelligence forces.

The infinite range of variations is also one of the code book's greatest disadvantages. Only one code book need fall into enemy hands for almost every agent to be in danger, for decoding messages then presents no problem.

The German cruiser Magdburg. When the Russians passed her codebook to the British, the Admiralty's Room 40 was able to decode German naval signals.

In 1914 one of the most famous instances of this occurred. The German cruiser *Magdburg* ran aground and came under fire from a Russian warship. Later, the Russians recovered the body of a German seaman, who still held a code book in his arms. The book came into the possession of the British, and soon they were able to understand German naval signals. Although there is still disagreement about who won the great naval battle of Jutland, one wonders how it might have turned out if the British had not had this advantage.

An even more striking instance was that of Pearl Harbour. American Intelligence had access to Japanese code books just prior to the bombing of Pearl Harbour in 1942, and it is now known that had the American agents only been more successful in putting two and two together, the raid might have been thwarted.

Of course, the reason for the great outcry over the bombing of Pearl Harbour arose from the fact that the attack came before the declaration of war. The Japanese had not, in fact, actually intended this, although they *had* intended that the attack should immediately *follow* the handing of the declaration to the American Secretary of State. However, the declaration had been sent in code to the Japanese Embassy and the cipher staff had to decode it in time to present it at 1 p.m. in Washington. But by the time it was received, decoded and delivered it was nearly 2.30 and the attack had been timed to begin about an hour before. Surely this is one of the tensest dramas in cryptology, for during the same hours American intelligence staff were decoding and attempting to get to the chiefs of military and naval staff partly decoded messages indicating that war was on the way. The warnings were too late, to some extent because their

At the battle of Jutland, the British had information on the movements of the German fleet because they had cracked their wireless code. But the British ships also used flags to co-ordinate their movements.

(see next page) Pearl Harbour was attacked before the Declaration of War reached the American President in Washington.

urgency was not understood. So by a combination of circumstances in handling and intercepting codes, the fleet at Pearl Harbour was not warned, was undefended in the air, and did not even put to sea before the attack began.

The risk of one captured code book leading to the collapse of a whole spying operation, is overcome to some extent by the use of small spy-rings, a dozen or less men working together in a group. Each ring uses a different code book, which means that if one ring is discovered, others are not automatically in danger. Of course, communication between rings becomes difficult; each must work through headquarters, but this can also be an advantage.

When codes are used, a possible safeguard against the capture of an agent and his code book leading to the fall of several other agents might be to issue every agent in the field with an individual code book. Although Gabriel di Lavinde was able to do just this for twenty-four of Clement's agents, the system is too awkward and slow for modern use and is not employed by any of the major Intelligence services such as the American CIA, the Russian KGB, Australia's ASIO and the British Secret Service, recognised as the world's most secretive intelligence and counter-intelligence services. It is simply not practicable to issue hundreds, perhaps thousands, of agents with different code books and handle the huge volume of decoding that would result.

So we arrive at what is probably the most widely used system of disguising messages — the *cipher*. A *code* involves the replacement of a *word*, a *phrase* or even an entire *sentence* by a code equivalent. A *cipher* goes one step further and replaces each individual *letter* with a secret equivalent.

There are two basic types of cipher. One is the *transposition cipher*. In this, the order of the letters of the message is re-arranged to hide the meaning. This can be achieved in many ways. The message

REINFORCEMENTS NEEDED

might be re-arranged by writing it backwards

DEDEEN STNEMECROFNIER

The more words there are in the message, the more effective is this system of transposition. An even simpler rearrangement is to run the words into each other

REINFORCEMENTSNEEDED

Again, the more words in the message, the more effective the system. Then, these ideas can be combined, running words into each other backwards

DEDEENSTNEMECROFNIER

To hide the normal breaks between words, the message can be arranged into groups of letters

REIN FORC EMEN TSNE EDED

or, backwards

DEDE ENST NEME CROF NIER

The message might be broken into groups of three, four or five letters and each group reversed

REI NFO RCE MEN TSN EED ED

IER OFN ECR NEM NST DEE DE

Now these could run into each other

IEROFNECRNEMNSTDEEDE

or the entire message could be reversed

EDEEDTSNMENRCENFOREI

Other possible re-arrangements exist, like

FLEET BASED AT PLYMOUTH

LFEET ABESD TA LPMYUOHT

Here the first two letters are reversed, the third and fourth are reversed and so on. In words with an odd number of letters, the last letter might be left at the end, or be brought forward

FLEET BASED AT PLYMOUTH

TLFEE DABES TA LPMYUOHT

Both Julius Caesar and the Emperor Augustus used ciphers that have survived to this day.

or arranged to fall in the middle or in the second or fourth position. As long as the recipient knows, the choice is as wide as the number of letters in a word.

FLEET BASED AT PLYMOUTH

LFTEE ABDES TA LPMYUOHT

LTFEE ADBES AT LPMYUOHT

LFETE ABEDS TA LPMYUOHT

To make the transposition more effective, any one of the above arrangements can be combined with a grouping of letters

FLEET BASED AT PLYMOUTH

LFEET ABESD TA LPMYUOHT

LFEE TABE SDTA LPMY UOHT

LFE ETA BES DTA LPM YUO HT

LF EE TA BE SD TA LP MY UO HT

These groups again can be run into each other

LFEETABESDTALPMYUOHT

and backwards

THOUYMPLATDSEBATEEFL

So even a simple transposition cipher has many alternative possibilities. Nevertheless, this type of cipher is only a poor second to the *substitution cipher* for variety. In substitution ciphers, each letter of a given message is substituted or replaced by some entirely independent letter or symbol. Often this simply involves the use of a different alphabet, just as in a foreign language words are sometimes 'transliterated', for example, English names are often transliterated into the Cyrillic or Russian alphabet.

Perhaps the simplest substitution is to use the alphabet backwards

A B C D E F G H I J K L M N O P Q R S T U V W X Y Z

Z Y X W V U T S R Q P O N M L K J I H G F E D C B A

This renders the message

ENEMY ADVANCING SEND HELP

as

VMVNB ZWEZMXQMT HVMW SVOK

Numbers can be used to make a simple variation

A B C D E F G H I J K L M N O P Q R S T U V W X Y Z
1 2 3 4 5 6 7 8 9 10 11 12 13 14 15 16 17 18 19 20 21 22 23 24 25 26

or

A   B   C   D   E   F   G   H   I   J   K   L   M
26 25 24 23 22 21 20 19 18 17 16 15 14

N   O   P   Q   R   S   T   U   V   W   X   Y   Z
13 12 11 10 9   8   7   6   5   4   3   2   1

The first gives the enciphered message

E   N   E   M   Y   A   D   V   A   N   C   I   N   G
5   14 2   13 25 1   4   22 1   14 3   9   14 7

S   E   N   D   H   E   L   P
19 5   14 4   8   5   12 16

The second you can work out for yourself.

An interesting variation numbers is to represent letters with Roman numerals

A	I	H	VIII	O	XV	V	XXII
B	II	I	IX	P	XVI	W	XXIII
C	III	J	X	Q	XVII	X	XXIV
D	IV	K	XI	R	XVIII	Y	XXV
E	V	L	XII	S	XIX	Z	XXVI
F	VI	M	XIII	T	XX		
G	VII	N	XIV	U	XXI		

Now the message reads

V	XIV	V	XIII	XXV	I	IV	XXII	I	XIV	III
E	N	E	N	Y	A	D	V	A	N	C-

IX	XIV	VII	XIX	V	XIV	IV	VIII	V	XII	XVI
I	N	G	S	E	N	D	H	E	L	P

Julius Caesar's cipher was imitated and refined through the centuries. In its simple form it involves moving each letter of the alphabet three places to the right

A B C D E F G H I J K L M N O P Q R S T U V W X Y Z
X Y Z A B C D E F G H I J K L M N O P Q R S T U V W

So

BRITONS BEATEN AT LONDON

would read

YOFQLKP YBXQBK XQ ILKALK

The Emperor Augustus, from whom we get the name for the month of August, used a similar cipher.

A B C D E F G H I J K L M N O P Q R S T U V W X Y Z
B C D E F G H I J K L M N O P Q R S T U V W X Y Z A A

We do not know why Augustus chose AA instead of A to represent Z for the A would have been equally effective.

The message

SEND SOME BRITONS TO ROME

would be

TFOE TPNF CSJUPOT UP SPNF

An endless number of variations of the basic idea behind these two Roman ciphers is possible. The alphabet may be moved any number of places to the right, as in Caesar's cipher, or to the left, as in Augustus' cipher.

To make it more complicated, one can move so many places in one direction and then so many in the other. Below, A has been moved three places to the right, B one place back, C three places to the right, D one back, and so on

A B C D E F G H I J K L M N O P Q R S T U V W X Y Z
Y Z B A D C F E H G J I L K N M P O R Q T S V U X W

The message

HAVE TAKEN ENEMY STRONGHOLD

is enciphered

EYSD QYJDK DKDLX RQONKFENIA

and the variations are almost endless.

Another basic idea with a host of possible variations is the *random selection system*. Simply write out the alphabet and then select, at random, any one letter to represent another letter. Here are just four possibilities

```
A B C D E F G H I J K L M N O P Q R S T U V W X Y Z
E T A O N R I S H D L G C M U F Y P Z W B K V L X Q
J F U A L D I Y M B N E Q W C Z G X H R V K T S P O
R H V A J Z M C O U D F Q X E S I K W L G N T Y B P
Q W E R T Y U I O P A S D F G H J K L Z X C V B N M
```

Now the message

HAVE TAKEN ENEMY STRONGHOLD

may be enciphered in any of the following forms

	SEKN	WELNM	NMNCX	ZWPUMISUGO
or	YJKL	RJNLW	LWLQB	HRXCWIYCEA
or	CRNJ	LRDJX	JXJQB	WLKEXMCEFA
or	IQCT	ZQATF	TFTDN	LZKGFUIGSR

Random selection operates equally well if we substitute the letters of the alphabet with numbers

```
A   B   C  D   E   F   G   H  I   J   K  L   M
17  23  5  18  20  24  21  9  15  16  1  19  4

N  O  P  Q   R   S   T   U   V  W   X   Y   Z
6  7  8  10  11  12  26  25  3  22  2  14  13
```

and the cryptogram now is

```
H   A   V  E         T   A   K  E   N        E   N  E   M  Y
9   17  3  20        26  17  1  20  6        20  6  20  4  14

S   T   R   O  N  G   H  O  L   D
12  26  11  7  6  21  9  7  19  18
```

41

In these random selection ciphers we see the first serious attempts to produce cipher machines which can select a random cipher far faster than the human brain. Early devices used simply rotating alphabets.

The great Italian architect, Leon Battista Alberti, born in 1404, was a friend of the Pope's talented secretary, Leonardo Dato, whose work included ciphers. Probably it was through Dato that Alberti became interested in cryptology, and about 1466 he wrote the essay that contained one of the central ideas of modern cryptography. This is the basic idea of *polyalphabetic substitution*. With it, almost any conceivable arrangement of the alphabet can be used as a basis for substitution, and can be changed as often as you wish.

The diagram shows the very simplest form of the cipher machine sometimes called the Alberti Disc.

Turn the inner disc till any letter of your choice is opposite A. This is the *key letter*. The discs remain in this position for the duration of the present cryptogram. Find each letter of your message on the inner alphabet and its cipher equivalent will be the letter opposite it in the outer disc. Take the message

NEED HELP

and set key letter E opposite A. As the first letter of the message is N, find N on the inner disc. This gives M. The next two letters are both E: again locate E on the inner alphabet and read off the N opposite. D is opposite O; H opposite S; E is again N; L is opposite G and P is opposite F. The enciphered message reads

MNNO SNGF

Make your own cipher disc from card. Cut two discs as shown, and the cursor centred on the top drawing. Pin together. To encipher, choose any suitable start position, and rotate the cursor to find your plaintext letters on the outer ring. Read off cipher equivalents on the inner ring.

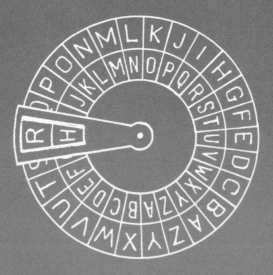

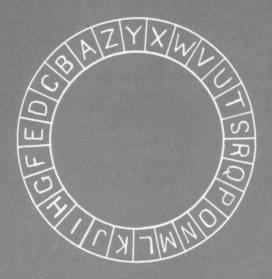

1 *Charles Wheatstone, a professor of philosophy at King's College, London. His "cryptograph" was displayed at the Exposition Universelle in Paris in 1867.*

2 *Charles Babbage, English mathematical genius, "the father of the computer", who used algebra to solve cryptograms. A friend of Wheatstone and Playfair, and one of the great minds of modern British cryptology.*

There is no reason why A should be kept opposite the E for the next cryptogram. If the inner disc is turned to another position this gives a new cipher.

From this simple start, cipher devices grew more complicated, giving a greater variety of possible cipher alphabets. From the rotating inner disc and the motionless outer one, the idea of two rotating concentric discs came about. The discs bore standard alphabets reversed to each other. The device works in much the same way as its forerunner.

Alberti's basic idea was developed further by an American, Decius Wadsworth, in 1817. However, the British scientist, Sir Charles Wheatstone, in 1867 invented what is now generally known as the *Wheatstone Cipher Device*, and received the credit for this development.

Wheatstone's cipher machine also has two concentric alphabets. But the outer alphabet, arranged in the normal ABC order, contains an extra space, indicated + in our diagram.

The purpose of this space is to allow a *null*, a meaningless letter, to be selected automatically to fill the normal spaces between words. (It has another useful effect which is explained below.) The inner alphabet is jumbled in a random order.

Two hands are centred like clock hands on the disc, and, like clock hands, are connected through gears so that they move at different rates.

In use, the long hand and short hand are placed over each other both pointing to the blank space. The long hand is moved in turn to each of the letters of the message to be enciphered, and the geared connection moves the short hand to a corresponding cipher letter, and these are

WHEATSTONE'S OWN DESCRIPTION OF THE PLAYFAIR CIPHER, MARCH 26, 1854

Specimen of a Rectangular Cipher

```
m b p y a
d q z g f
r n h s e
u t k v i
l w c o x
```

A despatch in the above cipher preserving the separations of the words:

We have received the
xn epis erxhgfrf knr

following telegraphic despatch
gxaabytet inxrdsexekp frhybiph

A despatch in the same cipher with no external indication of the separation of the words:

We have received the
xnzuyinferxhgfrfvgeh

following telegraphic despatch
itmyymxtsqgvrxsfemhpkxxitsexckwh

The same cipher arranged in a different rectangle:

```
m b p y a d q z g
f r u h s e j u t
k i i l w c o x -
```

We have received the following telegraphic despatch
cs sycr usswbpab feh jkddaquck fhchbtrwnty hynasgle

Key to the permuted alphabet employed in the preceding cipher

```
magnetic
bdfhjklo
pqrsuvwx
yz
```

m b p y a d q z g f r n h s e j u t k v i l w c o x

Signed   C. Wheatstone.

45

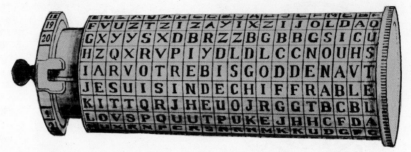

written down in order. At the end of each word the long hand is brought again to the blank space, and the letter shown correspondingly by the short hand is also written down, thus hiding the word space.

A random cipher can be selected by moving one disc to bring the key letter of one's choice opposite any other letter, or the blank space. The cipher is changed by changing the rate at which the small hand moves relative to the big one. For example, movement of a single space by the big hand might be accompanied by an equal movement of the small hand. Alternatively, the machine can be set to give a corresponding movement of three, four, five or any number of places forward.

The endless possibilities are clear: the two discs can be arranged in any order and the changes of relative movement of the hands are numerous.

Eighteen ninety-one saw a new type of cipher device. The great French cryptologist, Army officer and official cryptanalyst, Etienne Bazeries, invented a *cylindrical cipher machine* consisting of twenty alphabets. This machine is the basis of modern practical *polyalphabetic substitution* systems. Bazeries shares the credit for this invention with the famous Thomas Jefferson, who described a very similar device, using thirty-six alphabets, in his papers now preserved in the Library of Congress. Jefferson called it a 'wheel cipher', because it is made up of as many as thirty-six wheels on a central shaft. Bazeries' *cylindrical cipher* consists of twenty discs on a central shaft, each disc having a different arrangement of the alphabet around its edge. To encipher a message, the cryptographer arranges the first twenty letters of his message along a given row. (The rows are numbered for

Take a wooden cylinder
about 50 mm in diameter
and about 200 mm long.

On the ends, divide the
circumference into 26
equal parts (each will be a
little less than 14 degrees).

Join these divisions with
parallel lines along the
side of the cylinder. Now
the outside of the cylinder
is divided into 26 equal
parts.

Cut the cylinder into
twenty discs of equal
thickness.

Make a table of twenty
jumbled alphabets, and
print one around the edge
of each disc.

Take a thin bolt of
suitable length, drill a
corresponding hole
through the centres of the
discs and assemble them
on the shaft.

Make a numbered disc for
the end, so that you can
locate any row when the
discs are fixed in a given
position by tightening
the screw.

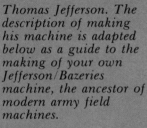

*Thomas Jefferson. The
description of making
his machine is adapted
below as a guide to the
making of your own
Jefferson/Bazeries
machine, the ancestor of
modern army field
machines.*

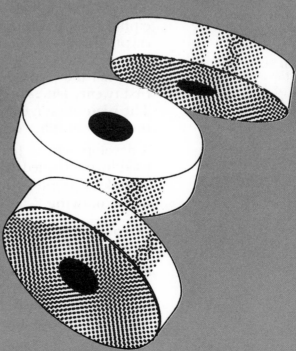

47

The St. Cyr cipher. Based on the simple principle of sliding alphabets and developed by the famous French military college of the same name, this is one of the most effective simple ciphers.

To make a St. Cyr cipher take two strips of white cartridge paper, one about 3 cm wide and 20 cm long, and the other 1 cm wide and 40 cm long.

Cut a slot in the shorter strip long enough to fit a normal alphabet above it.

Write in the alphabet.

ABCDEFGHIJKLMNOPQRSTUVWXYZ

XWVUTSRQPONMLKJIHGF BA ZYXWVUTSRQPONMLKJIHGFEDCBA Z VUTSR

Cut two slits 1 cm deep as marked.

Take the long thin strip and write on it two reversed alphabets, and pass the strip through the slits.

Select a key letter, say S. Slide the strip till S is under A.

Read off cipher letters below the clear letters.

convenience.) The coded version may then be read off from any one of the other rows. The procedure is repeated for the next twenty letters of the message, the coded version being read off the *same row* as previously.

To read the message, the recipient needs an identical cipher machine and must know which row the cryptographer read off. Assuming that the cryptographer has used the jumbled alphabet of, say, the third row, to encipher the cryptogram, the recipient must arrange the first twenty letters of the cryptogram along the third row. The plain message then appears along the same row that the cryptographer originally used.

A development of Jefferson's and Bazeries' machines was used by the United States Army from 1922 onward. How to make a simple cylindrical cipher machine is described in the drawing.

Of course, the wheels may be rearranged in a different order and alignment almost as often as you wish.

From these humble beginnings, cipher machines have developed till today they are complex devices, often electrically operated. Many not only encipher messages, but also transmit and decipher the messages.

48

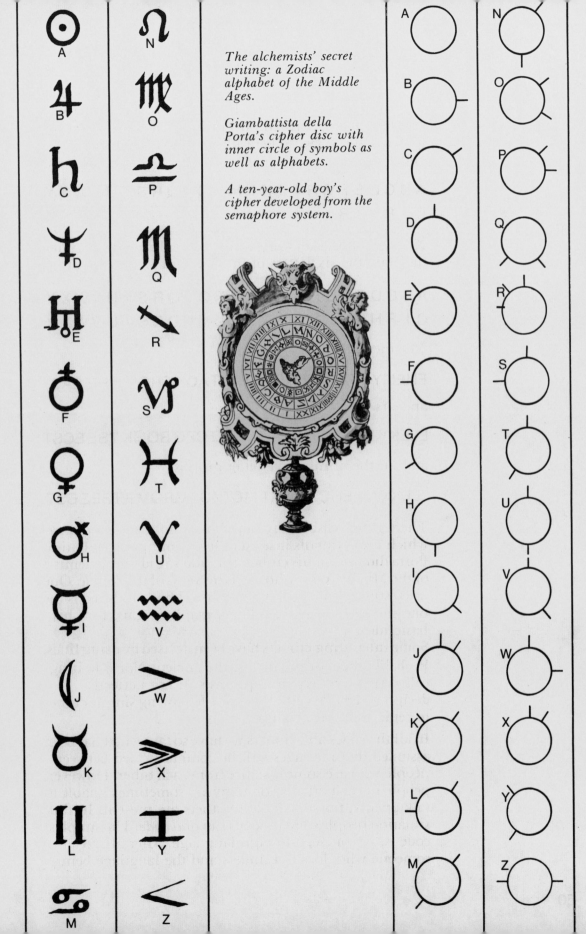

The alchemists' secret writing: a Zodiac alphabet of the Middle Ages.

Giambattista della Porta's cipher disc with inner circle of symbols as well as alphabets.

A ten-year-old boy's cipher developed from the semaphore system.

A popular variation of the random selection system, is the use of a *keyword* to rearrange the alphabet. Any word can be used as the key, although it is usual to employ words which do not repeat letters. Take the word CIPHER itself. The alphabet is written out, in its normal order. Now spell out the keyword beneath the alphabet, C under A, I under B

A B C D E F G H I J K L M N O P Q R S T U V W X Y Z
C I P H E R

Now follow the keyword with a normal alphabet, leaving out only the six letters of the keyword as they occur.

A B C D E F G H I J K L M N O P Q R S T U V W X Y Z
C I P H E R A B D F G J K L M N O Q S T U V W X Y Z

The message

ENEMY PREPARING TO ATTACK FROM THE EAST

appears as

ELEKY NQENCQDLA TM CTTCPG RQMK TBE ECST

and, in the normal five-letter groups

ELEKY NQENC QDLAT MCTTC PGRQM KTBEE CST. . .

There is no reason why one should not devise a cipher which uses symbols instead of letters or numbers. Batista Porta did this on his cipher disc, and so did the alchemists of the Middle Ages, who used the Signs of the Zodiac. One interesting idea which a ten-year-old boy produced is the one shown on page 49. The semaphore gave him his basic idea.

Some interesting ciphers have been devised by using lines. Probably these originated in the ancient Norse writing called runes, where inscriptions still not perfectly deciphered used symbols like the following simple cipher to replace the runic alphabet.

In all the codes and ciphers we have so far seen, it has been assumed that messages will be communicated between people who are some distance from each other. However, people in each other's company are sometimes unable to talk openly, possible because others are present. In this situation people sometimes use an *oral code*. The simplest code is, of course, a foreign language. After all, to someone who does not understand the language being

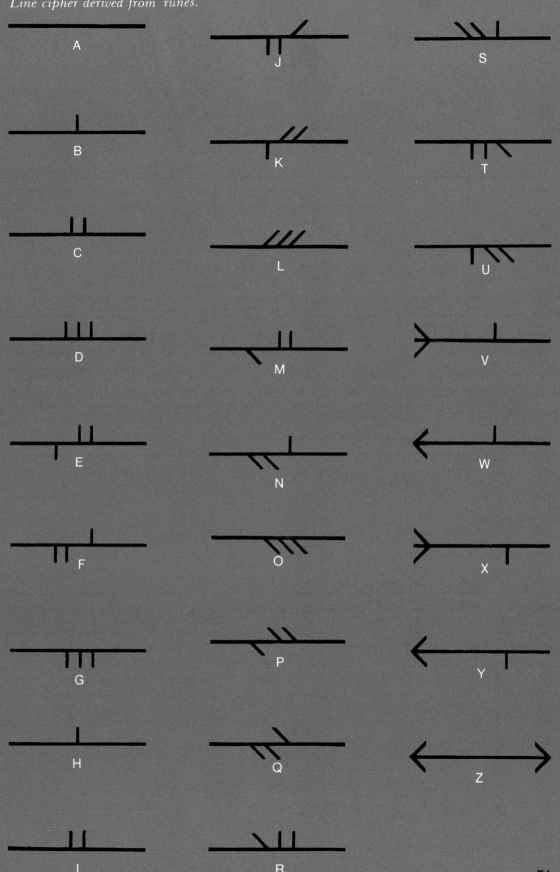

Line cipher derived from runes.

51

Ansur : Asa, God

Thurs : Giant

Wynn : Comfort

Feu : Cattle

Ur : Bison

Ken : Torch

Nied : Necessity, thraldom

Is : Ice

Rad : Cartwheel

Geofu : Gift

Hagall : Hail

spoken, it is all mumbo-jumbo. When people happen to speak the same foreign language the problem of secret communication sometimes is solved.

Not everyone can master a second language — some even seem to have trouble mastering their native tongue, but it is possible, for simple messages, to invent a secret language. Schoolboys and prisoners have used secret words for centuries, and some of these have later become quite ordinary parts of the language.

A simple way to begin is to invert each word, so that

MEET ME AT SEVEN

becomes

TEEM EM TA NEVES

Two other schoolboy techniques were common. One was to add -*ski* to the end of every word spoken

MEETSKI ATSKI COFFEESKI BARSKI LATERSKI

Many English-speaking schoolboys have used 'Pig Latin'. Basically this adds the digraph UP to words

wUPill yUPou gUPo tUPo tUPhe lUPeft

Although it appears simple in print, this language is actually quite difficult, not only to learn but also to understand.

Now that you can make and read some codes and ciphers you may like to make a simple experiment in transmission. High-speed radio transmission is used in all aspects of modern espionage. It is not uncommon to squeeze 500 words into two seconds of tape by the use of high-speed recording and transmission techniques, which may of course be used for both plain and ciphered messages in speech or in morse code.

For those who own a two-, or preferably three-speed tape-recorder and a telephone, the following experiment may be interesting. Record your message on the lowest speed and then telephone a friend who owns a tape-recorder with similar speeds (it may help if all this is arranged beforehand). The message is played back at the highest speed and recorded by the receiver at the same speed. To read the message, it has only to be played back at the original recording speed.

And with that we have reached the end of this first section.

2

Samuel Morse is well known as the inventor of the electric telegraph, by which most of our telegrams and cables are sent. In the late 1830s he developed Morse Code. Morse gave the shortest sign, the dot, to the most frequently used letter, E. By generally following this basic principle of cryptography, he was able to develop such a simple, concise code, that modern International Morse Code is still only slightly different from his original.

The modern electric telegraph is the result of the work of Charles Wheatstone (of the Wheatstone Cipher) and William Cook in Britain and Morse and his assistant Alfred Vail in the United States. Since April 1, 1845, when Morse telegraphed a message between Washington and Baltimore, the telegraph line and cable have carried countless secret and non-secret messages in war and peace — plain language, business code and secret cipher — in morse code. The story of telegraphic communications from that point on is one of almost uninterrrupted advance.

Morse code rapidly became the international language of modern communications. In England, one of the first police messages ever radioed was the one which caused the arrest of the murderer, Crippen, who was on board a ship for escape to the United States. In Australia, the Overland Telegraph, completed in the last quarter of the nineteenth century, enabled morse telegraphy to link Australia with Britain by joining the international cable system at Darwin. During both world wars, dramatic messages like the SOS from the torpedoed *Lusitania* went out in morse. The best known and most universally used non-secret code today is morse code.

In most of the ciphers commonly used, each letter of the alphabet is replaced by another letter or by a number.

Banjoewangi
Nov: 30th 1871

Mess: Clark & Forde,

Gentlemen

Completion of Cable

I write to inform you that the British Australian Cable was successfully completed on the 19th instant You will receive this Mail the detailed log and Abstract also Copies of the tests made on board ships at Port Darwin and here; and of the tests so far, of the land Cable

Arrived at Port Darwin

We arrived at Port Darwin with Captain Halpin and others in the Investigator on the 30th October The Edinburgh and Hibernia were already there —

Tests at Port Darwin

Careful tests were taken of such of the Cable on board the two Ships as it was intended to lay the other pieces have since been tested here and are all in good condition. These tests were necessarily

and

made on board ship and with a Marine galvanometer — They are therefore not quite so satisfactory for the short pieces of Cable as those that were made at Singapore from the Wharf

remarks on same

The temperature of the Tanks a few days before our tests, was considerably below the temperature of the air. The Tanks were necessarily emptied in order to get the eyes in order and filled up with very hot water from Port Darwin Harbour. — the calculated value of the insulation for the S.S. Hibernia at 75° F is therefore probably above the true value.

The value given from the Copper resistance

is probably the more accurate. The insulation was remarkably high of the Cable generally — one piece only was a little doubtful, the 8.043 knots of Type B. The deflection obtainable on a marine galvanometer with the longest

Appendix to the final report of the officers of the cable crew to their principals in London.

Officers of the Telegraph Construction and Maintenance Company who laid the international cable from Darwin to Banjeowangi, in eastern Java.

Laying cable to New Zealand, at Botany Bay in February 1876.

The Overland Telegraph Line linked Australia with the rest of the world by the use of Morse Code. Here the first pole is planted in Darwin on September 15, 1870.

1 *The modern semaphore code with hand flags.*

2 *The wig-wag code. Morse can be signalled as rapidly as ten to fifteen words a minute with hand flags.*

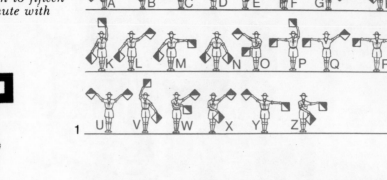

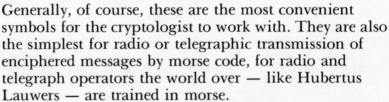

1

2 *start*

dot

dash

Generally, of course, these are the most convenient symbols for the cryptologist to work with. They are also the simplest for radio or telegraphic transmission of enciphered messages by morse code, for radio and telegraph operators the world over — like Hubertus Lauwers — are trained in morse.

Flags are also used to transmit morse. An outstanding example is the wig-wag system, used by most English-speaking navies, and also by Boy Scouts. Two hand-held signal flags are used. They are held and moved as shown in the drawings, and a skilled signalman can send morse in this way very rapidly, even as many as ten to fifteen words a minute. The *semaphore code* illustrated is another widely used flag code.

Morse had first to reduce the spoken language to a form which could be transmitted and received as electrical impulses. The resulting system of dots and dashes is in reality the earliest form of what today is termed *data transmission.*

Despite the obvious advantages of the telegraph, it was handicapped for many years by the fact that the operator had to encode and decode the messages into morse and plain text, in his own handwriting. This limited the rate of transmission and reception to around forty words per minute. This is about the *minimum* typing speed required for secretarial work. Then, at the turn of the present century, Charles Wheatstone invented an automatic transmitter which could transmit morse at up to 400 words per minute. Messages still had to be decoded by the operator.

In the 1920s, a New Zealand telegraph engineer, Murray, invented a new system, which used a typewriter keyboard instead of the old morse code key. A corresponding

A	●▬	N	▬●
B	▬●●●	O	▬▬▬
C	▬●▬●	P	●▬▬●
D	▬●●	Q	▬▬●▬
E	●	R	●▬●
F	●●▬●	S	●●●
G	▬▬●	T	▬
H	●●●●	U	●●▬
I	●●	V	●●●▬
J	●▬▬▬	W	●▬▬
K	▬●▬	X	▬●●▬
L	●▬●●	Y	▬●▬▬
M	▬▬	Z	▬▬●●

The early mechanical semaphore as used for rapid communication in France and across Europe during the wars of Napoleon. The different positions of the arms indicated letters or figures, and this gave the basis for later commercial codes like the ABC and Bentley's.

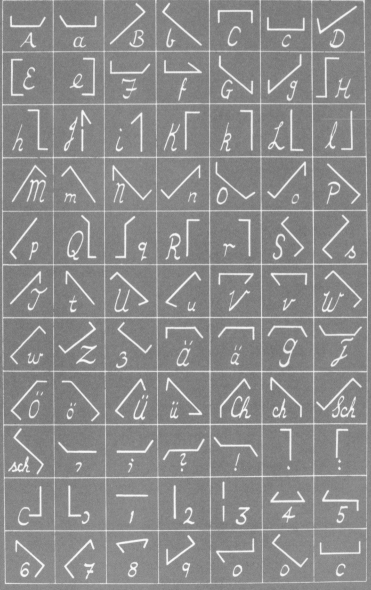

A pocket Morse key as used on the construction of the Overland Telegraph Line in the 1870s.

Samuel Morse. He devised the most widely used of all codes— International Morse Code.

machine at the other end received and typed out the messages. This was the beginning of the modern *teleprinter,* and *telex* is now used almost as widely as telegrams and cables for direct communication between business offices around the world.

International telegraph traffic grew so rapidly from Morse's work that business, postal and diplomatic organisations were soon spending millions of dollars on this form of communication. Modern multi-national business companies developed rapidly as international trade and oil development for industry took place from about the middle of the nineteenth century. Soon they were spending vast sums on communications, and the demand for codes suitable for the telegraph developed out of the combined need for secrecy and economy.

The first code associated with Morse, published in 1845, was designed for *secret* communication — in fact it was called *The Secret Corresponding Vocabulary, Adapted for Use to Morse's Electro-Magnetic Telegraph,* by Francis Smith. But businessmen in America were already devising their own dictionary-type codes. In Europe, number groups had long been used for various mechanical semaphore systems based on similar principles to the one just described, and these were taken over or adapted for business.

Before and after World War I a great deal of traffic between Britain, Australia, and other European nations and their colonies took place, often over prices of land, oil shares and mining rights, raising of loans for development and so on.

This traffic needed to be regulated so that the international cable network could operate efficiently, and

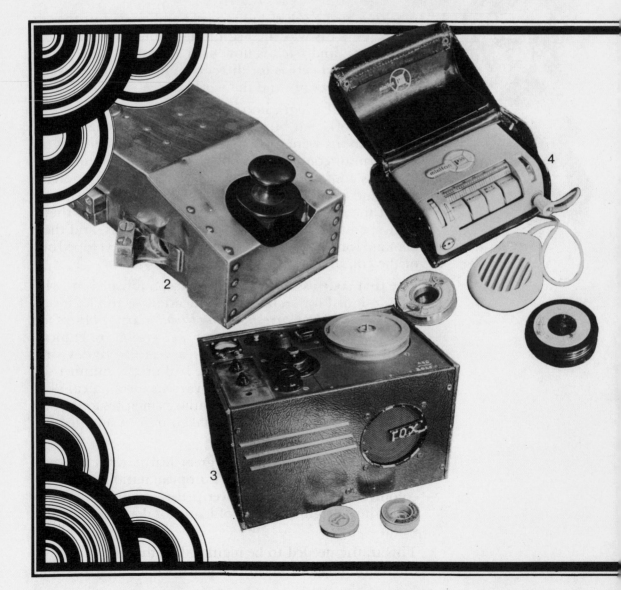

1 *A corner of the A.W.A. Transmitting Centre at Pennant Hills, Sydney, in the 1920s.*

Early communications equipment.

2 *Morse key in a brass case, about 1902. Navy pattern No. 310, it was used in early experimental wireless telegraphy.*

3 *Pyrox Wire Recorder, 1945. Used a spool of fine stainless-steel wire which gave about one hour of recording time.*

4 *Minifon pocket wire recorder, 1955.*

5 *"Midget" Portable Disc Recorder. Used by ABC War Correspondent (Technician) L. Edwards in war zones in World War II.*

6 *Early Morse key. Note the code on black bakelite.*

7 *Early transmitter as used by the ABC in New Guinea.*

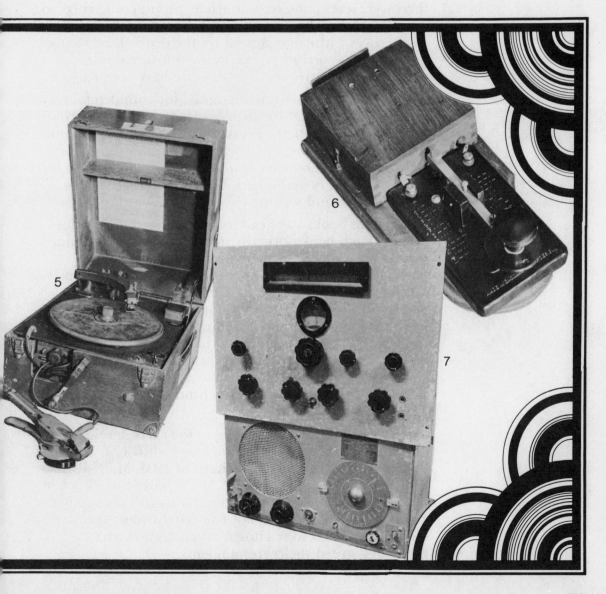

1

there were several international telegraphic conferences to agree on basic codes and charges for sending them. These conferences ultimately agreed on the general use of five-letter codes — a further reason for transmission of messages in the five-letter groups we have seen earlier.

Very soon, codes specially designed for commercial use were developed, and for many years were widely used in international business. Typical codes were the Marconi, the Bentley, and the ABC. As the examples show, these were simply dictionaries of invented five-letter words for most common business expressions, names of places, money units, and so on.

Large code books were published and sold to business houses. Each book normally included a key and an index so that encoding was made easier by referring to a particular subject, like *mining*, for example. Obviously, number groups could be used as well as code words. Although these are certainly not secret codes, they were often used as well to restrict knowledge of the messages to the few that knew the codes or had copies of the code books. They could be, and in fact often were, used as simple secret codes by taking the codeword an agreed number of places ahead of or behind its normal place in the tables.

An interesting example related to the early development of British interests in Australia was *Cahill's Stock and Station Code* published in Britain in 1904. Many British companies owned land in the Australian outback when wool was the major export commodity of value to both countries. Before the days of five-letter codes, any dictionary words were chosen and assigned whatever meanings suited the correspondents.

Code No.	Code Word		Code No.	Code Word	
81823	UDSEV	DISCOUNT(S) (See Allowance, and Bill)	81894	UDXNO	DISCOUNTING
4	UDSHY	All discounts	5	UDXOP	Bills for discounting
5	UDSIZ	At what rate can you discount	6	UDXTU	DISCOURAGEMENT
6	UDSJA	At what rate can you discount 30 d/s bills on	7	UDXUV	DISCOURAGING (See Advice)
7	UDSNE	At what rate can you discount 60 d/s bills on	8	UDXYZ	DISCOVER(ED) (See Ascertain, and Recover)
8	UDSOF	At what rate can you discount 90 d/s bills on	9	UDXZA	DISCOVERY
9	UDSSI	At what rate can you discount 6 m/s bills on	81900	UDYAD	DISCREDITED
81830	UDSUK	Brokers discount rate of —%	1	UDYBE	DISCREPANCY (See Difference, and Deficiency)
1	UDSYO	Buyer requires further discount of —%	2	UDYCF	Serious discrepancy
2	UDTAT	Can discount at	3	UDYDG	DISCRETION (See Careful)
3	UDTBU	Can discount at 1% over bank rate	4	UDYEH	Acting on own discretion
4	UDTEX	Can you discount bills (on —) ; if so, at what rate	5	UDYFI	Cannot give discretion
5	UDTFY	Cannot allow discount	6	UDYGJ	If allowed discretion
6	UDTHA	Cannot discount bills (on —)	7	UDYHK	Left to discretion of
7	UDTIB	Cannot discount except at high rates	8	UDYIL	Left to my (our) discretion
8	UDTLE	Cash discount	9	UDYJM	Left to your discretion
9	UDTOH	—% discount	81910	UDYKN	May I (we) act on own discretion
81840	UDTPI	2½% discount	1	UDYLO	Will use discretion
1	UDTUM	5% discount	2	UDYMP	DISCRIMINATION (See Choice)
2	UDTWO	10% discount	3	UDYNR	DISCUSS (See Consult)
3	UDTYR	Discount at bank rate	4	UDYOS	To discuss the matter
4	UDUAV	Discount at —% over bank rate, but in no case	5	UDYPT	To discuss the matter with me (us)
5	UDUBW	Discount brokers [at less than 5%	6	UDYRU	DISCUSSED (See Considered)
6	UDUCX	Discount of —% allowed	7	UDYSV	Not discussed
7	UDUDY	Discount of —% allowed if paid within one month of date	8	UDYTW	Was it discussed
			9	UDYUX	DISCUSSION (See Board Meeting, etc.)
8	UDUEZ	Discount rate for (—) bills on	81920	UDYVY	After discussing
9	UDUFA	Discount rate for 30 d/s bills on	1	UDYWZ	Before discussing
81850	UDUGB	Discount rate for 60 d/s bills on	2	UDYXA	For future discussion
1	UDUHC	Discount rate for 90 d/s bills on	3	UDYYB	DISEASE (See Illness, etc.)
2	UDUID	Discount rate for 6 m/s bills on	4	UDYZC	Foot and mouth disease
3	UDUJE	Do not discount bills on	5	UDZAF	DISENGAGED (See Engaged)
4	UDUKF	Easier at —% discount	6	UDZDI	Disengaged to the extent of
5	UDULG	Extra discount(s)	7	UDZEJ	If not disengaged
6	UDUMH	Extra discount of —% per cash	8	UDZIN	DISH(ES)
7	UDUNI	Firmer at —% discount	9	UDZJO	DISHONEST
8	UDUOJ	Full trade discounts	81930	UDZOU	DISHONOURED (See Acceptance, Bill, and Draft)
9	UDUPK	Higher rate of discount	1	UDZTY	DISINCLINATION (See Inclined)
81860	UDURL	I (we) will accept discount rate of —%	2	UDZUZ	DISINFECT(ANT)(S))
1	UDUSM	If you can discount	3	UDZVA	Disinfectant fluid
2	UDUTN	If you cannot discount	4	UDZYD	Disinfectant fluid coefficient
3	UDUVP	Less discount of —%	5	UDZZE	DISINTEGRATOR(S) (See Grinder)
4	UDUWR	Less usual discount(s)	6	UEABM	Disintegrator for (—) to treat — tons per day
5	UDUXS	Lower rate of discount	7	UEACN	(—'s) patent disintegrator
6	UDUZU	May I (we) discount bills on	8	UEADO	DISINTERESTED (See Interested)
7	UDUZU	No discount(s)	9	UEAFR	DISLIKED
8	UDVAX	Owing to increased demand for discounts	81940	UEAGS	DISLOCATED (See Communication)
9	UDVBY	Owing to less demand for discounts	1	UEAHT	DISLOCATION (See Navigation, Part I)
81870	UDVEB	Showing all discounts (See Invoice, Part I)	2	UEAJV	Owing to dislocation
1	UDVHE	Slightly higher rate of discount	3	UEAKW	DISLOYAL
2	UDVIF	Slightly lower rate of discount	4	UEALX	DISMANTLED
3	UDVLI	Subject to usual discount(s)	5	UEAMY	DISMANTLING
4	UDVOL	Trade discount(s)	6	UEANZ	DISMISSAL
5	UDVSO	Usual discount(s)	7	UEAPB	After dismissal
6	UDVUR	What are full discounts	8	UEARC	Before dismissal
7	UDVXU	What discount allowed	9	UEASD	Due to dismissal of
8	UDVYV	What further discount for cash	81950	UEATE	DISMISSED
9	UDWAZ	What is rate of discount	1	UEAVG	DISMISSING
81880	UDWBA	DISCOUNT MARKET (See Money)	2	UEAWH	DISOBEDIENCE
1	UDWED	Easier tone in discount market	3	UEAXI	DISOBEYED (See Command, Part I)
2	UDWFE	Firm tone in discount market	4	UEAYJ	Disobeyed orders
3	UDWIH	Firmer tone in discount market	5	UEAZK	DISORDER(S)
4	UDWJI	In discount market dealings were chiefly for	6	UEBAN	DISORGANISED
5	UDWON	Weaker tone in discount market	7	UEBBO	DISORGANISING
6	UDWPO	What is the tone in discount market	8	UEBES	DISPARITY (See Difference)
7	UDWUT	DISCOUNTABLE	9	UEBFT	DISPATCH (See Despatch)
8	UDWVU	Not discountable	81960	UEBGU	DISPENSABLE
9	UDWYX	DISCOUNTED	1	UEBIW	DISPENSE WITH
81890	UDWZY	Discounted bill(s) (See Bill)	2	UEBKY	Can dispense with
1	UDXAB	Have discounted	3	UEBMA	Can you dispense with
2	UDXEF	Have not discounted	4	UEBOC	Cannot dispense with
3	UDXHI	Have you discounted	5	UEBRE	Dispense with (—) if possible
			6	UEBUH	DISPENSED WITH
			7	UEBVI	If dispensed with
			8	UEBYL	If not dispensed with

NOTE. Discount rates can sometimes be more closely expressed by using the Number Tables (Units and fractions).

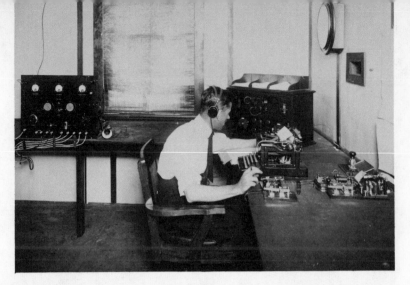

With the development of teleprinter services, these codes have generally fallen into disuse. The teleprinter can, of course, also use plaintext or codewords or figure groups.

All of us live every day of our lives with one code or another, and usually with several. These codes surrounding our daily lives are not basically intended to conceal anything from us, but to make life somewhat easier for the general community. The international postal system is probably the world's largest user of non-secret codes. In addition to morse, it uses a large number of *place* and *identification* codes. These are essential for mail delivery as well as teleprinter services and so on.

There are only a small number of people to whom the phrase 'of no fixed abode' can be strictly applied. Even the nomadic tribes that wander the vast expanses of the Sahara Desert settle at recognised oases and many other such tribes often reside within closely defined territories. Those of us in our 'Western Civilisation' usually live in a house or a flat, and the post office has to find us there.

The *Postal Code* is an increasing world-wide practice which has now been with most of us for so long that we ignore it or take it for granted. As its name suggests, it is a *code* not a cipher. Each postal code has a particular meaning, readily understood by anyone who knows how to decode it. As with secret codes where the use of a *code book* is essential, many Post Offices nowadays issue their own code books in order to assist the delivery of mail by having the relevant codes included in addresses.

Postal codes work by dividing the country into large postal areas, each area being assigned a general code. The larger areas are then sub-divided. Often an individual town is a sub-division, although where the population is sparse, or in remote areas, several small townships may be included in the one sub-division. At the other end of the scale, a large town or city may contain several sub-divisions. The codes given to sub-divisions and the main divisions are linked. The main division's code number or letter usually forms the initial part of the sub-division code.

The United States of Americal uses a five-digit postal code — the Zip Code — probably the best-known postal code in the world. The main postal divisions are not the fifty States, for each State contains a number of main divisions.

The Golden State, California, is America's third-largest State in area and second-largest in population density. My research on California's postal codes, conducted on a codebreaking basis with the aid of American journals, indicates that California has at least five major postal divisions. An area in the south surrounds the town of San Diego and stretches west and as far north at least as Santa Ana. From Santa Ana to the southern half of Los Angeles is another division which also includes the western suburbs of Los Angeles. West of Los Angeles another area centres on the town of Fresno. A further major division is centred around the country rather than the city of San Francisco, while a fifth appears to be based on the county of Sacramento, whose city of Sacramento is the capital of California.

This much can be learnt by studying a number of American journals and a map of California. Readers may find it amusing and perhaps educational to tackle postal codes of other areas along similar lines. Maps present no problem and journals from the United States, France, Germany and Britain are available in most English-speaking countries. The journals are used simply for the advertisements, which give addresses with code numbers.

Each of the five Californian areas identified has a two-digit code. Code 90 denotes the division to the south and west of Los Angeles; 91, the division to the north of Los Angeles; 92, the division based on San Diego; 93, the division to the west around Fresno; 94 is San Francisco and 95 is Sacramento. Although each of these five divisions has 9 as its initial digit, 9 does not denote California, for 98 denotes Washington.

Within each of these major divisions are numerous sub-divisions. For example, Western Avenue, in the city of Los Angeles, is 90047, while South Western Avenue, again in Los Angeles, is 90004. Hawthorn, a small township to south of Los Angeles is 90250.

POSTCODE ➤

In division 91, North Hollywood is 91607 and Burbank 91503. San Diego, in division 92, is coded as 92041 and 92120, obviously for different areas of the city.

San Francisco is 94101, Sacramento is 95813, and so it goes on. The famous bootlegging city of Chicago, for example, is 60639, the first two digits, 60, being one of the Illinois codes.

Australia has adopted a digital postcode, using only four numbers. The main postal divisions are the States (the Australian Capital Territory sharing with New South Wales and the Northern Territory sharing with South Australia). Each State is allotted an initial digit as the State code and all sub-divisions (usually towns) within that division have a postal code which commences with that digit.

The State codes in Australia are:

New South Wales and Australian Capital Territory (ACT)	1
Victoria	2
Queensland	3
South Australia and Northern Territory	4
Western Australia	5
Tasmania	6
	7

Each sub-divisional code starts with the initial digit of the State; the following three digits denote the postal district and the place of destination.

For example, a postcode commencing with the digit 4 belongs to Queensland. The second largest State in Australia, Queensland covers vast areas. From Brisbane to Birdsville, Cairns or Mount Isa are all fantastically long distances. So more information comes from the second digit. All 40 and 41 initial digits, for example, denote the Brisbane postal district. This is still not enough, for the city spreads over a large number of suburbs. To pin-point the suburb, the last two digits are added. While 4000 is the city proper, 4013 denotes Northgate, 4102 denotes Wooloongabba and 4020 denotes the City of Redcliffe, a separate city, nevertheless within the Brisbane postal district.

The British postal code system is somewhat more complicated partly because the larger cities like London, Liverpool, Manchester and Birmingham had postal codes of their own long before the general introduction of the

---

QLD.

HOME HILL 4806
Homestead 4816
Hopevale 4871
Horseshoe Bay 4816
Howard 4659
HUGHENDEN 4821
Humpybong 4019
Hungerford 4493

I (QLD.)
Ibilbie 4741
ILFRACOMBE 4727
Imbil 4570
INALA 4077
INDOOROOPILLY 4068
Indooroopilly Centre 4068
INGHAM 4850
INGLEWOOD 4387
INJUNE 4454
Inkerman 4806
INNISFAIL 4860
Innot Hot Springs 4872
IPSWICH 4305
Iron Range 4871
Ironside 4067
Irvinebank 4872
Irvingdale 4404
Isis Central Mill 4660
ISISFORD 4731
Isle of Capri 4217

J (QLD.)
Jackson 4426
Jambin 4702
JAMES COOK UNIVERSITY 4811
JANDOWAE 4410
Japoonvale 4860
JERICHO 4736
Jimboomba 4280
Jimbour 4406
Jimna 4515
Jindalee 4074
Jondaryan 4403
Jones' Hill 4570
Julatten 4880
JULIA CREEK 4823
JUNDAH 4736

K (QLD.)
Kabra 4702
Kaimkillenbun 4406
Kairi 4872
Kalapa 4702
Kalarka 4702
Kalbar 4309
Kalinga 4030
Kallangur 4503
Kalpowar 4680
Kandanga 4570
Kangaroo Point 4169
Karara 4370
Karragarra Island 4165
Karumba 4891
KEDRON 4031
Kelso 4815
Kelvin Grove 4059
Kenilworth 4574
KENMORE 4069
Kennedy 4816
Keperra 4054
Kepnock 4670
Keppel Sands 4703
Kidston 4871
KILCOY 4515
Kilkivan 4600
KILLARNEY 4373
KINGAROY 4610
Kingsthorpe 4400
Kingston 4205
Kin Kin 4571
Kippa-Ring 4020
Kirra 4225
Kleinton 4352
Kogan 4406
Kokotungo 4702
Kolan South 4659
Koongal 4701
Koonkool 4702

L (QLD.)
Labrador 4215
LAIDLEY 4341
Lake Clarendon 4343
Lamb Island 4165
Lamington 4285
Landsborough 4550
Laravale 4286
Laura 4871
Lawes 4345
Lawnton 4501
Leyburn 4361
Limevale 4384
Linderman 4741
Lindum 4178
Linville 4305
Littlemore 4680
Loch Lomond 4370
Loganlea 4205
Lone Pine 4069
Longford Creek 4805
Long Island 4800
LONGREACH 4730
Loreto Hill 4151
Lota 4179
Lower Nudgee 4014
Lower Tully 4854
Lowmead 4676
LOWOOD 4311
Lucinda 4850
LUTWYCHE 4030
Lyra 4351
Lytton 4178

M (QLD.)
Macalister 4409
MacGregor (Qld.) 4109
Machans Beach 4871
MACKAY 4740
McKINLAY 4830
Macknade 4851
Maclagan 4403
Macleay Island 4165
Macrossan 4816
Maidenwell 4315
Main Beach 4215
Makowata 4670
MALANDA 4885
Malbon 4824
MALENY 4552
Ma Ma Creek 4347
MANLY (QLD.) 4179
Mansfield 4122
Many Peaks 4680
Mapleton 4560
Marathon 4821
Marcoola Beach 4564
Marburg 4346
MAREEBA 4880
MARGATE BEACH 4019
Marian 4741
Marlborough (Qld.) 4705
Marmor 4698
MAROOCHYDORE 4558
Martynvale 4870
MARYBOROUGH 4650
Mary Farms 4880
Mary Kathleen 4824
Maryvale 4370
MATER HILL 4101
MAXWELTON 4830
Mayne 4006
Mc—see Mac
MEANDARRA 4422
Meeandah 4008
Memerambi 4609
Mena Creek 4860
Merinda 4805
Meringandan 4352
MERMAID BEACH 4218
Miallo 4873
Miami 4220
Middle Ridge 4350
Midgee 4702

QLD.
Milton 4064
Milton Centre 4064
Mingela 4816
Mirani 4741
Miriam Vale 4677
Miriwinni ...
Mission ...
MITCHELL ...
Mitchelton ...
Miva ...
Moffat ...
Moggill 4069
Molloy ...
Mondurran ...
Monduran ...
Monkland ...
MONTO ...
Montville ...
Moolboolaman ...
Mooloolah 4553
Moonie 4406
Moore ...
Moorina ...
MOORE ...
Moorland ...
Moranbah ...
Morayfield ...
Morella ...
Moresby ...
Moreton ...
MORGANVILLE ...
Morningside ...
MORVEN ...
MOSSMAN 4873
Mount Abundance ...
Mount Beppo ...
Mount Berryman 4341
Mount Coolon 4804
Mount Coot-tha ...
Mount Cotton ...
Mount Crosby ...
Mount Fox ...
Mount Gravatt ...
Mount Larcom ...
Mount Morgan ...
Mount Perry ...
Mount Surprise 4871
Mount Sylvia 4343
Mount Walker ...
MOURA ...
Mourilyan ...
Muckadilla ...
Mudgeeraba ...
Mudjimba Beach ...
Mulgildie 4630
Mulgowie ...
Mullett Creek ...
Munbilla ...
Mundowran ...
Mundubbera ...
MUNGALLALA ...
Mungar ...
Murarrie ...
MURGON 4605
Murphys Creek ...
Murray Upper ...
Mutarnee ...
Mutchilba ...
MUTTABURRA 4732
Myrtlevale ...

N (QLD.)
Nagoorin ...
NAMBOUR 4560
NANANGO ...
Narangba 4504
Nashville ...
Nathan ...
NEBO ...
Nelia ...
Nelly Bay ...
Nerang ...
Netherdale 4741
Newell 4873
NEW FARM 4005
Newmarket 4051
NEWSTEAD (QLD.) 4006
Nikenbah ...

QLD.
Noosa Heads 4567
Noosaville 4566
Normanby 4059
Norman Park 4170
Northgate ...
Northlands 4350
NUNDAH 4012

O (QLD.)
O'Connell ...
Ooralea ...
Oonoonba ...
Oriel Park ...
Oxford Park 4053
Oxley 4075
Oxley Central 4075

P (QLD.)
Pallas Street 4650
PALM BEACH (QLD.) 4221
Palm Beach North 4221
Palmwoods ...
Park Avenue 4701
Parkhurst ...
Parramatta Park 4870
Peachester 4519
Peak Crossing 4305
Peel Island 4163
Peeramon 4872
Pialba 4655
PIMPAMA ...
Pinbarren ...
Pinkenba ...
Pioneer ...
PITTSWORTH ...
Pleystowe ...
Point Lookout ...
POMONA ...
Port Douglas ...
PROSTON ...
Pullenvale ...
Pumicestone 4510

Q (QLD.)
QUNABA ...

R (QLD.)
Raby Bay 4163
Racecourse Mill 4741
Raceview 4305
Raglan 4697
Railway Estate 4810
Rainbow Beach 4570
Ravensbourne 4352
RAVENSHOE 4872
Ravenswood 4816
Redbank 4301
REDCLIFFE 4020
Redhill ...
Richmond ...
Riverview 4305
ROCKHAMPTON NORTH 4701
Rocklea 4106
Rockville 4350
Rosedale ...
Roma ...
ROCKHAMPTON ...

S (QLD.)
ST. GEORGE 4393
St. Johns Wood 4060
St. Lawrence 4671
St. Lucia South 4067
SALISBURY 4107
Saltern 4730
Samford ...
SANDGATE (QLD.) 4017
Sapphire 4702
SARINA 4737
Sarina Beach 4737
Scarborough 4020
Scarness 4656
Scotts Point 4019
Seaforth 4741
Selheim 4816
Seven Hills (Qld.) 4170
Severnlea 4351
Sharon 4670
Sherwood 4075
Shorncliffe 4017
Silkwood 4856
SOUTH BRISBANE ...
SOUTH BRISBANE ...
SPRINGSURE 4722
STANTHORPE ...
SURAT 4417
SURFERS PARADISE 4459
Sunshine Beach 4567
Sunrise 4470

T (QLD.)
TARGINNIE ...
TAROOM 4420
Tarragindi 4121
Tarzali 4872
Tekowai 4741
Teneriffe 4005
Tennyson 4105
THARGOMINDAH ...
THEODORE 4719
The Summit 4377
Thinoomba 4650
Thompson Estate 4103
Toobeah ...
Toogoolawah 4313
Toombul 4012
Toonpan 4816
Toorbul 4510
TOOWONG 4066
TOOWOOMBA 4350
Torbanlea 4662
Torquay 4657
Torrens Creek 4816
Torwood 4066
TOWNSVILLE 4810
TOWNSVILLE MIL. P.O. 4813
Traveston 4570
Trebonne 4850
Trinity Beach 4871
Tugun 4224
TULLY 4854
Tumoulin 4872
Tungamull 4703
Turallin 4357
Twin Hills 4721

U (QLD.)
Upper Mount Gravatt ...
Upper Stone 4850
Upper Yarraman 4314
Urandangie 4824
Urangan 4658

W (QLD.)
Wacol ...
Walkerston ...
Wallon Bridge 4061
Walton Bridge 4061
Wamuran 4512
Wandal 4700
Watalgan 4670
Waterford 4206
Wavell Heights 4012
Weipa 4874
Wellcamp 4350
Wellers Hill 4121

Y (QLD.)
Yaamba 4704
Yalboroo 4741
Yalleroi 4736
Yamala 4702
Yandaran 4673
Yandina 4352
YANDINI 4854
Yangan 4371
Yarabah 4736
Yarraman 4871
YARRAMAN ...
Yarwun 4694
Yatala 4207
Yeerongpilly 41..
Yengarie 4650
YEPPOON 46..
YERONGA 41..
Yorkeys Knob 41..
YULEBA 4427
YUNGABURRA ...

Z (QLD.)

SOUTH AUSTRALIA.

A (S.A.)
ADELAIDE (CI...)
Private Boxes...
G.P.O. 5000
Rundie St...
5000
Adelaide North ...
ALBERTON 50...
Aldgate 5154
Aldinga 5173
Aldinga Beach ...
Angaston 5554
Gardens East 5401
5554
ANGASTON ...
Angle Park ...
Angle Vale 51...
Appila 5480
Andrews 5455

Other Queensland entries (central columns, partial)
WINDORAH ...
Windsor (Qld.) ...
WINTON 41...
WOODFORD ...
Woodgate 4660
Woodridge 41..
Woorim ...
Woody Point 40..
WOOLOONGABBA 4102
Wulgura 4811
Wutul 4352
Wyandra 4489
Wyberba 4351
Wycarbah 4702
Wynnum 4178
WYNNUM CENTRAL 4178
Wyreema 4352

Post codes in action. Which letter goes into which chute? Electronic sorting equipment and postcodes work together to speed deliveries.

system. London has long been divided into postal districts, simply because of its size and large population. Letters used to be addressed to London WC2 or London N16, and so on. With the general introduction of postcodes, the British Government attempted to combine the old London codes with the new postcodes. Today, one might address a letter to London WC1 V6JS, whereas previously London WC1 would have been sufficient. Where previously London N17 would serve, the code for a particular part of the former N17 district today is N17 8NT. In both cases, the old code is included in the new, no doubt simplifying delivery of letters coded both ways, as must inevitably occur.

Britain does not have States or Provinces, but uses smaller administrative units known as Counties, or, in larger towns, County Boroughs. The larger counties are sub-divided for administrative and historical reasons. Yorkshire is made up of Ridings: West Riding, East Riding and the North Riding, plus a number of County Boroughs, but postal codes do not always follow these units.

The small town of Rugeley, in Staffordshire, lies approximately eight miles south of Stafford, the County Seat, and eight miles north of the Cathedral City of Lichfield. One would expect the code for Rugeley to have some link with one or the other of its larger neighbours, yet, for postcode purposes, it has been linked with the town of Walsall, in south Staffordshire. The Walsall general code is WS. Rugeley, a sub-division within the Walsall postal district, is 15, and WS15 denotes Rugeley. The town is large enough to warrant further coding: WS15 2BX and WS15 2TX pinpoint the districts of the author's former home and the present home of his family — at opposite ends of Rugeley.

Since 1876, when Alexander Graham Bell invented the telephone, an increasing number of people have accepted into their lives yet another non-secret code — the telephone number. Unlike postal codes, telephone numbers have achieved international uniformity, in that all telephone codes, on the STD (Subscriber Trunk Dialling) system, are totally digital. Where letters are still dialled first, these are, of course, simply three other numbers, as the older telephone dials show. When dialling a Knightsbridge number, the first three letters involved — KNI — are in effect 453.

Every private telephone subscriber has his own private number, but the STD user must also note the *code* for his district and for his general area. In Australia, Brisbane telephone users have the *Area Code*, 072, followed by the code numbers for their particular suburb, say, 84 for Redcliffe, and finally the private number. A similar system operates throughout the STD world. In the United States, for instance, 201 puts the caller through to a particular area in the State of New Jersey, and 201-943 takes the call through to the New Jersey town of Ridgefield. In Britain, 01 is the Area Code for London, while 01-804 puts the call through to the Enfield district of London.

Senders of telegrams will have noted that the telephone service uses a phonetic alphabet, again a kind of accepted and recognised code

A	Alfred	N	Nellie
B	Benjamin	O	Oliver
C	Charles	P	Peter
D	David	Q	Queen
E	Edward	R	Robert
F	Frederick	S	Samuel
G	George	T	Tommy
H	Harry	U	Uncle
I	Isaac	V	Victor
J	Jack	W	William
K	King	X	X-Ray
L	London	Y	Yellow
M	Mary	Z	Zebra

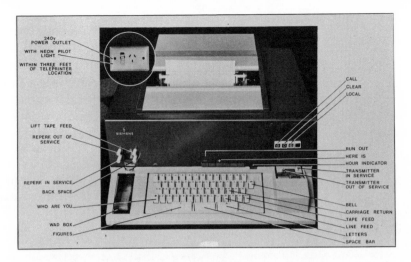

The teleprinter or TELEX.

This offers a quick way of checking spellings when telegrams are lodged by phone.

As the long-term aim of introducing STD is to link the world together for the users of the telephone, a knowledge of the telephone area codes of other countries would be useful information to have at hand. The collection of telephone area codes could be tackled in exactly the same manner as described for postcodes.

By the 1950s the teleprinter, the modern result of Murray's system, had become the workhorse of post office telegraphy. By that time, telegram traffic was growing so rapidly that post offices found they needed to be linked directly to each other to handle the increased volume. The TRESS system was developed to fill this need. TRESS (Teleprinter Reperforator Exchange Switching System) usually has an automatic switching centre in every major city or central telegraph office, and TRESS offices scattered throughout the country. Each office has its own three-letter code. For example, QTE might route messages to Townsville in Queensland.

To send a telegram by TRESS, an operator types out the code address and completes the message, and the rest is left to electronics. At the switching centre, sophisticated equipment recognises the coded address, stores the message and transmits the telegram to the receiving teleprinter when the line is free.

At about the same time as the post office was beginning to appreciate the advantages of direct communication between offices, the business world was asking for a more convenient system of transmitting messages. To accommodate this, the TELEX system was introduced. Telex is operated in much the same way as the telephone, but words, not sounds, are transmitted.

Each subscriber is given a code number, like a telephone number, but consisting of five figures. To call another subscriber, the operator presses the *call* button on the teleprinter and after receiving a GA (go ahead) signal, types the code number of the subscriber being called. The distant teleprinter answers by printing its 'answer-back' code, which consists of the called subscriber's telex number and name.

The telex system has its own service code, printed out to the caller if the called number cannot be connected

NC	no circuit
DER	called service out of order
OCC	called service occupied
ABS	subscriber absent
NA	access not admitted
NP	called number is not a connected service

Today, telex is the means used almost universally for direct contact between the international offices of large companies. Improvement of telegraphy has not ceased with the teleprinter. With the computer now an established fact of life, it was perhaps inevitable that eventually someone would devise a general communications system incorporating the use of the computer — the electric brain. One of the latest means of transmitting messages is DATEL, a word made up from the initial digraph of *data* and the initial trigraph of *tele*communications; or, if you prefer, *digital transmission*.

The speed of measurement of digital transmission is in *bits-per-second*. Datel averages around 1200 bits-per-second, the equivalent of 25 words per second, but on special lines can manage up to 48,000 bits-per-second, or around 1000 words per second. A *bit*, incidentally, comes from the fact that the computer uses a two-digit (binary digit-bit) code.

Before leaving the Post Office and its wide use of non-secret codes, it is perhaps worth mentioning that not only sounds and words, but also pictures, drawings, photographs, plans, and so on can, nowadays, be sent from one corner of the world to another.

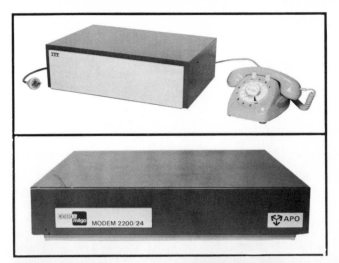

A DATEL unit.

Operator at Carnarvon Coastal Radio Station uses both morse and voice.

1 Telemetry Tracking Command and Monitoring Station for Intelsat Satellites above Pacific and Indian Oceans.

2 Dish with 97-foot parabolic antenna communicates with control in the US via Pacific Ocean satellite.

3 Artist's impression of the Intelsat IV communications satellite. Orbiting 36,000 km above the earth, Intelsat is capable of carrying approximately 6000 simultaneous two-way telephone conversations or up to twelve simultaneous colour TV transmissions.

4 Listening to messages from space–Mills Cross radio telescope.

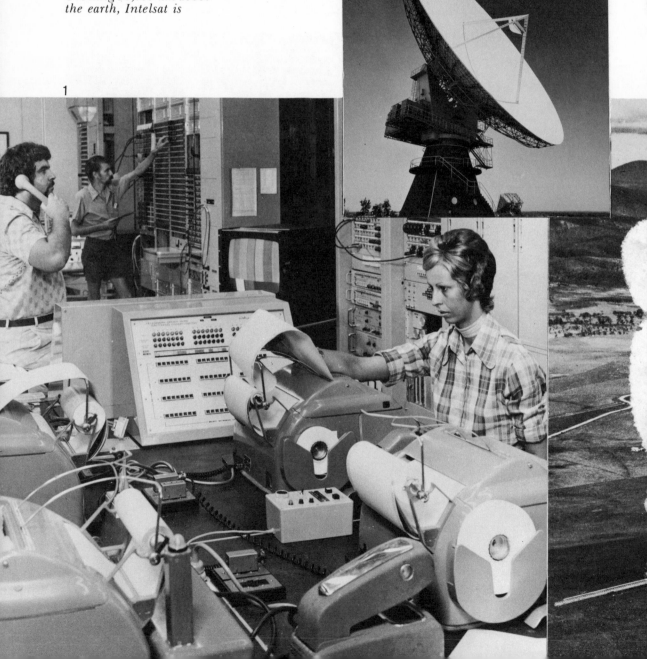

3

4

Codes are all around us.
What is CX-3?
Autoidentity:
Whose car is which?

Which State or Territory?

Government departments
have their own symbols.

Even road-rollers have
identity.

The post office is by no means the only user of non-secret codes. Anyone who does his own car repairs has encountered this. To buy most articles it is enough simply to go to the appropriate store, look around, and order. Not with automobile spare parts! To buy any mechanical part — from a simple gasket to a synchro hub — you order the part and the storeman then checks the relevant serial number in one book. This tells him whereabouts in the store the part is likely to be kept. Nor does it end there. Having found the part, the storeman then has to check through yet another book to locate the price. In both procedures he is checking the code.

If you need to identify the paint used on your car, look under the bonnet. You will not find the name of a colour, but a code letter. With Ford Escorts, for example, S is the code for a particular shade of yellow.

The motor-car also has coded registration plates. In Australia, for example, even the basic colour pattern of these plates is a simple code. Cars from Queensland, Victoria and the Northern Territory use white figures — and letters — on a black background: South Australia and Western Australia use the reverse, black figures on a white background: Tasmania and the Australian Capital Territory use blue figures on a white background and New South Wales uses black figures on a yellow background. Even at a quick glance, one can distinguish the State of registration. Australian registration plates go a step further in distinguishing cars of one State from cars of another State. The use of white figures on a black background is a colour pattern shared by two States and one territory, but further coding exists in the order of the letters preceding the number. Queensland registrations commence with N, O or P (and Q on trucks and trailers); the Northern Territory uses digital registration only and Victoria uses the letters, J, K, and L.

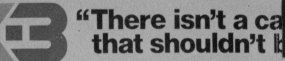

CX-3 "There isn't a car on the road that shouldn't be using it."

Codes might help to recover a stolen bike.

Foreign visitor?

How to find a bike in a crowd.

Car registrations in Britain go a little further. To begin with, there is no colour code with plates. White figures on a black background dominate, with black figures on a yellow background beginning to take preference simply because of the slightly superior qualities of legibility of that particular combination. Nevertheless, those who know how to read the British registration codes can tell where the vehicle was registered, and with vehicles manufactured after 1962 it is even possible to tell the age of the vehicle.

British registration plates have three letters followed by three numbers. Since 1963, a fourth letter has been added at the end of the numbers to denote the year of registration. An A denotes a vehicle made between August 1, 1962 and July 31, 1963; B denotes a vehicle made between August 1, 1963 and July 31, 1964, and so on, with the exception that the letters I, O, Q and Z are not used in this position. Any vehicle without this added letter has been manufactured before 1963.

To determine a vehicle's place of registration in Britain one has to note the second or the second and third letters of the registration. Complications, however, do exist. For example, London and the Scottish town of Kirkcaldy share the XA series; London and Luton share the XD series; London and Torbay share the XF series. Other complications arise from a limitation being placed on certain licensing authorities, such as Staffordshire which has the BF series, but only the CBF to HBF, the JBF to PBF, the RBF to TBF and the VBF to YBF; the others being allotted to another authority. The Essex County Council suffers from similar limitations: it has the WC series, but only the BWC to HWC, the JWC to PWC, the RWC to TWC and the VWC to YWC.

The Greater London Council has, of course, been allotted more index marks than any other British licensing authority. Some of the these are

1. LA to LY, except LC, LG, LI, LJ, LN, LQ, LS, and LV

2. MC to MY, except MI, MJ, MN, MO,MQ, MR, MS, MV, and MW

3. XA to XY, except XG, XI, XJ, XQ, and XS

4. YE to YY, except YG, YH, YI, YJ, YQ, and YS

International Registration Letters are a simple code which identifies the vehicle's country of origin. Many are straightforward and are known by almost everyone
AUS — Australia
CDN — Canada
GB — Great Britain
I — Italy
IND — India
J — Japan
MEX — Mexico
NZ — New Zealand
USA — United States of America

Others are fairly well known, even if their allotted index letters are perhaps not so obvious
CH — Switzerland
D — Germany
E — Spain
GBA, GBG and GBJ — Alderney, Guernsey, and Jersey (the Channel Islands)
GBM — the Isle of Man
GBZ — Gibraltar
NL — Netherlands
PL — Poland,
SF — Finland.

Others are more obscure, because they are rarely seen, but a copy of the United Nations 1949 Convention on Road Traffic — the International Registration Letters *Codebook* — solves most problems.

BH	British Honduras	RI	Indonesia	
BRG	Guyana	RIM	Mauritania	
BRN	Bahrain	RM	Malagasy Republic	
BRU	Brunei	RMM	Mali	
BS	Bahamas	RNR	Zambie	
CGO	Congo (Republic)	ROK	Republic of Korea	
CI	Ivory Coast	RSM	San Marino	
CS	Czechoslovakia	RSR	Rhodesia	
DY	Dahomey	RWA	Rwanda	
DZ	Algeria	SD	Swaziland	
EAK	Kenya	SME	Surinam	
ET	United Arab Republic	SN	Senegal	
HKJ	Jordan	SU	USSR (Russia)	
LB	Liberia	SY	Seychelles	
LS	Lesotho	TN	Tunisia	
MW	Malawi	V	Vatican	
PTM	Malaysia	WAG	Gambia	
RB	Botswana	WAL	Sierra Leone	
RC	Formosa (Nationalist China)	WD	Dominica	
RCB	Congo (Brazzaville)	WG	Grenada	} Windward Islands
RH	Haiti	WL	St Lucia	
		WV	St Vincent	
		YV	Venezuela	

```
0123456789  I: II'I III II"
```

Banks use codes in conducting their business, and the average customer would perhaps know best the codes used on cheques. These are simple two- or three-letter codes, which tell the customer something about his account. The actual account number is also, of course, a digital code. A few such simple letter codes are

CR — account in credit

CBK — cost of chequebook or duty stamp on cheques

or the one that brings a flutter to many a heart

DR — account overdrawn

still, perhaps, preferable to showing overdrawn amounts in red. (hence the phrase 'in the red.').

Other non-secret codes, are not always so prominent in the public's eye. Chess players have two codes by which they can record games, codes which are of interest only to other chess players. Masons have their own special marks which they etch onto stones; watch repairers mark a watch in special ways so as to know what repairs are required or what repairs have been carried out; even tramps have a code whereby they inform other tramps of the reception they are likely to receive at any house; manufacturers use codes. The list is almost endless — codes surround our everyday lives.

Most of us at some time come across the practice of coding retail prices. Clothing retailers especially seem to go in for coding. The customer picks up a jacket, reads the label which indicates the size, and so on, may also see a series of letters but no price clearly marked. To actually break the code is simple.

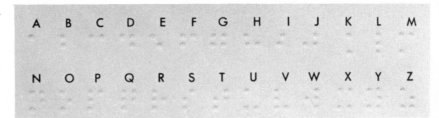

Mason's marks

Basically retail shops code by selecting a ten-lettered word or a number of words containing a total of ten different letters. Take the phrase THE FOX MARK. Each letter might then be numbered.

T H E   F O X   M A R K
1 2 3   4 5 6   7 8 9 0

An item of clothing priced, at say, $4.54c, would be marked

F/OF *or* **F.OF**

This works equally well with one ten-lettered word, so long as each letter is different

B L A C K R I D G E
1 2 3 4 5 6 7 8 9 0

An item of clothing priced at $13.67 would be marked

BA/RI *or* **BA.RI**

To break such a cipher (limited to digits, but cipher nevertheless) one simply has to find enough clothing to locate all ten letters, ask the shopkeeper the price of each item, and study the results.

Louis Braille, the son of a French saddler, was blinded with an awl when a child. This misfortune led to his devising the Braille alphabet, the internationally used system of raised dots over which blind people run their fingers.

In Braille, the International Distress Signal appears

S O S

Although most of us are fortunate enough to have little use for this cipher, huge numbers of books are transcribed into Braille and published for the use of the blind.

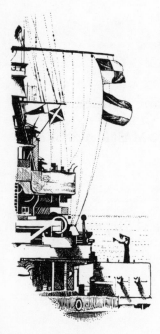

Signal flags properly hoisted.
For the International Flag Code see endpaper

The deaf and dumb alphabet too, is not secret. Anyone can learn it just as anyone can learn lip-reading. Both are ways to enable people handicapped by loss of speech or hearing, or both, to communicate with each other and with others who have learnt the system. The deaf and dumb alphabet is a *convenience code,* designed to make life easier for certain people who cannot communicate with normal speech.

Before leaving this introduction to non-secret codes and ciphers, the International Flag Code, must be mentioned. Coloured flags are used, and every ship carries a copy of the International Flag Code Book containing thousands of messages.

This code originated with the work of the famous Captain Marryat, in 1817, and has since been much developed by International Code of Signals committees.

Single letters signify common or urgent messages like insert code

G	I require a pilot
U	You are standing into danger
V	I require assistance
NO	I am on fire

As the Code Books are prepared in all important languages, the International Flag Code gives a reliable way of making immediate visual communication where language barriers or radio or other electronic equipment breakdown prevents the use of morse code.

Signal flags are usually hoisted singly, but if several must be shown they are read in this order

First — masthead
Second — starboard yardarm
Third — port yardarm
Fourth — triatic stay

Coloured lights perform a similar role at night if morse signalling with the signal lamp — the Aldis lamp — is for some reason impossible.

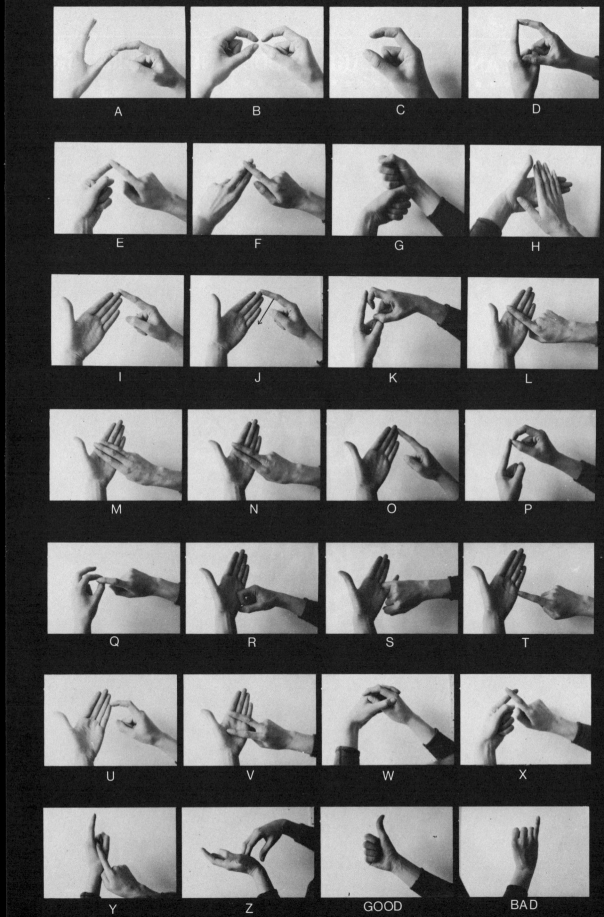

A B C D

E F G H

I J K L

M N O P

Q R S T

U V W X

Y Z GOOD BAD

3

There are no easy ways to crack a code or to break a cipher. No one has yet invented or discovered short cuts which will by-pass the hard work.

To break a cipher requires certain qualities on the part of the cryptanalyst. The first is the ability to study. Before anyone can hope to break a cipher, he must have a working knowledge of how ciphers are put together. Knowledge of how ciphers are compiled is an invaluable aid in decipherment. There may be a similarity between a system one has studied and the system one has to break. The wider one's knowledge of various cipher systems, the more likely it is that one will begin to recognise enciphered messages at a first or second look.

The second quality required is patience. Consider the story of the patience of the Arab cryptologist who contemplated an intercepted message to the Sultan of Morocco for fifteen years — about the year 1600 — before success was achieved!

A particular cipher may reveal nothing even after precious hours of searching for a clue. Good codes can be uncrackable, as can good ciphers. Short cryptograms with only a few letters or words often fall into this category. The only hope of breaking short enciphered messages is sometimes to know a little of the sender and intended recipient and accumulate a collection of messages from the one sender — in effect, to increase the length of the cipher.

The third quality required by the cryptanalyst is a vivid imagination. In breaking ciphers, one has to be prepared for almost anything and a good imagination helps, especially when the time has come to make wild, or calculated, guesses and nothing but imagination can hope to get answers.

With all this, the cryptanalyst needs luck! A little luck can bring answers which all the logical thinking in the world would never arrive at.

On encountering an enciphered message for the first time, one's immediate reactions may well be despair, panic and, hopefully, some determination. But somehow, some sort of sense must be made out of those crazy, mixed-up letters. Where to start?

Take the following message:

```
KN GBN AUZLVS QU WBUZ MUYB EUUW GVW
RPUQALVS UV JYVWGM VLSAQ FYQ LQ KLPP
FN G QBLRTM UZNBGQLUV GJ NVNCM GRQL
XLQM LV QAN GBNG AGJ LVRBNGJNW LV
QAN ZGJQ KNNT QANBN JAUYPW FN VU CUUV
QAGQ VLSAQ JU KGQRA UYQ EUB QAN
ZPGVN LQ KLPP CGTN UVN UXNBANGW
EPLSAQ GVW WZUB QABNN ZGBGRAYQNJ UV
LQJ BNQYBV
```

This may first appear impossible, but once the deciphering process is set in motion, step by step, the hidden meaning will slowly be revealed. We will assume the language is English.

Before starting to decipher any message, it is advisable to write out a *blank alphabet*:

A B C D E F G H I J K L M N O P Q R S T U V W X Y Z

Whenever a letter from the cryptogram is deciphered, write that letter down in its appropriate place beneath the blank alphabet. If it is discovered that X represents H, then X is written beneath the H. This serves two purposes. First, after having deciphered some six to eight letters, one may begin to suspect or even to see, a definite pattern: letters moved three places to the right, or some other pattern. Second, it is always advisable to keep a record of ciphers broken for the day may come when someone repeats a cipher and at some stage during the deciphering process the first example will be recalled. If a record of broken ciphers has been kept, the repeated cipher is simple to break.

The starting point in deciphering any cryptogram is to count the number of times each letter or other symbol has been used. So

A	16	H	0	O	0	V	17
B	15	I	0	P	8	W	9
C	3	J	9	Q	25	X	2
D	0	K	5	R	6	Y	7
E	3	L	17	S	4	Z	7
F	3	M	5	T	3		
G	20	N	26	U	21		

Every language in the world has its own particular and quite definite patterns. The English language is no exception. Among the twenty-six letters of the alphabet, letters such as Q, X and Z are used rarely, while other letters appear several times in one sentence. The list below arranges the alphabet according to frequency of use. The first letter is used more often than the second, the second more than the third, and so on. Such *frequency lists* come about from counting the use of each letter in passages containing 10,000 letters.

E T A O N R I S H L G C M U F Y P W B V K X J Q Z

By using the *letter-count* and the above frequency-list, we can start deciphering our cryptogram by assuming that as N appears more often than any of the other letters, then the chances are that the N has been used to replace E.

A word of warning! The *frequency-list* is based on averages, and therefore cannot be taken as a universally established truth. Although the E will most often be the most frequently used letter, there is still the chance that in some message this will not be true. Perhaps 90 times out of a 100, perhaps a little less, the T will come out second, the A third, but the top five letters do change their places in frequency order. This is one of the added difficulties in deciphering. The list should be used as a good general guide, but by no means an infallible one. It is a convenient starting point.

Having decided that N is E, now read through the enciphered message and place an E above, or below, every N.

```
KN GBN AUZLVS QU WBUZ MUYB EUUW GVW
 E   E
```

```
RPUQALVS UV JYVWGM VLSAQ FYQ LQ KLPP
FN G QBLRTM UZNBGQLUV GJ NVNCM
 E          E          E E
```

```
GRQLXLQM LV QAN GBNG AGJ LVRBNGJNW LV
          E   E        E E
```

```
QAN ZGJQ KNNT QANBN JAUYPW FN VU CUUV
 E     EE   E E      E
```

```
QAGQ VLSAQ JU KGQRA UYQ EUB QAN ZPGVN
                          E   E
```

```
LQ KLPP CGTN UVN UXNBANGW EPLSAQ GVW
         E   E   E    E
```

```
WZUB QABNN ZGBGRAYQNJ UV LQJ BNQYBV
      EE         E       E
```

This gives us several other leads, but before considering them, it is worth taking a closer look at a number of other clues which could have been used at the outset. These do not, however, always appear in messages, and certainly never in more complex cryptograms.

Take the seventh, tenth, thirty-fifth, thirty-sixth, and fifty-fifth letter groups, EUUW, UV, VU, CUUV and UV and consider three of these, EUUW, UV and VU. Take the four-letter group first; those two middle letters could be any one of a number of other letters, or could they? Try each letter of the alphabet in that position and it becomes obvious that the most likely are either EE or OO. As we have already deciphered N to be E, it must be possible for U to be O. UV and VU would have led us to a similar conclusion. As it is, these two will reinforce our decision. These two are unique, for of all two-letter words only *on* and *no* can be reversed in this way. Without EUUW, we would have been left with the problem of deciding whether U or V is O, but with the two clues together we now know that U is O and that V is N.

There is another letter which we could have come close to deciphering at the very beginning. The seventeenth group is simply G, alone. In the English language there are only two one-letter words, *a*, the indefinite article and *I*, the first-person singular. Therefore, G must be either A or I. A look at our *letter-count* shows us that G is one of the most common letters in this cryptogram. The third letter in the *frequency-list* is A. So we can start by assuming that G is A.

Having deciphered the E does give a number of leads. The first group of the cryptogram, KN, is now partly deciphered to read -E. The same is true of FN, now -E. Write out a list of all the two-letter words in use in the English language and it will become clear that there are four possibilities: *be, he, me, we*. Therefore K is either B, H, M or W; the same applies to F. A choice of four is a little too wide for us at this stage, but this clue should be kept in mind for later reference. If these were the only letters available, one would have to try each in turn and hope that some other light was cast from somewhere.

In our cryptogram there are three three-letter groups which end with E — GBN, QAN, and UVN. There are, of course, many words which could fit the bill, but the most common words in this category are the two words *the* (the definite article) and *are*. Again the choice at present is far too wide, but patience may soon bring in a further clue.

At this point, consolidate our knowledge of the cipher by filling in the blank alphabet

```
A B C D E F G H I J K L M N O P Q R S T U V W X Y Z
        A           E               O N
```

It is impossible to detect if any *pattern* exists yet. So, now read through the cryptogram again, filling in the newly-deciphered letters.

```
KN GBN AUZLVS QU WBUZ MUYB EUUW GVW
 E  AE  A E O N   O    O  O    OO  AN
RPUQALVS UV JYVWGM VLSAQ FYQ LQ KPLL
  O   N   O N  N A  N
FN G QBLRTM UZNBGQLUV GJ NVNCM
 E A    O E      ONA  E  E
GRQLXLQM LV QAN GBNG AGJ LVRBNGJNW LV
 A        N   E A EA A  N   E A E    N
QAN ZGJQ KNNT QANBN JAUYPW FN VU CUUV
  E A    EE     E E   O      E NO  OO
```

QAGQ VLSAQ JU KGQRA UYQ EUB QAN ZPGVN

  A N   O A   O   O   E   ANE

LQ KLPP CGTN UVN UXNBANGW EPLSAQ GVW

   A E ONE O E   EA   AN

WBUZ QABNN ZGBGRAYQNJ UV LQJ BNQYBV

   O   EE   A A   E ON   E N

Now we have several other clues that are worth considering. There is nothing further to help us yet with KN and FN, but, on the other hand, we can now decipher the definite article, *the*. Of the three possibilities, GBN, QAN and UVN, we have disposed of UVN, by deciphering the letters O, N and E, to give *one*. That leaves us with two possibilities, GBN and QAN. To the E of GBN we have added A, giving us A-E, which rules out *the*. So our three possibles have been reduced to one, QAN. Of course there is still the chance that QAN is not *the,* but some totally different word. We need to know if QAN contains T.

The *frequency-list* shows the T is the second most common letter in use and the early *letter-count* shows Q as the second most common letter in use in the cryptogram.

A little more than coincidence? It is almost certain that Q is T, which would make QAN, T-E. If we add A as H, we have THE and another letter deciphered.

Now return to the first of the original three possibilities for *the*, GBN. We ruled this out because G is A and, therefore, GBN now reads A-E. With only the middle letter missing, it should not be too difficult to find it. Try each letter of the alphabet in that space. We have eight words which could fit the bill; *ace, age, ape, ale, are, ate, awe* and *aye*. The last two we can discard as too obscure; *ale* is rather an old-fashioned word (it's beer nowadays), which leaves us with five. Of those five, the most frequent and therefore the most likely, is *are*. This gives us B as R.

The eighth group should now be considered, GVW. There are only three letters that could fit in that end gap; D (*and*), T (*ant*) and Y (*any*). T we have already deciphered, so our choice rests between W = D or W = Y. Of these, the first, giving *and* is far more common. We can assume that W is D.

The twenty-third group, LV, also offers food for thought. LV has been partly deciphered to read -N. The two-lettered words ending with an N are, *an, in* and *on*. L would appear to be A, I or O. However, we already know that G is A and that U is O, leaving us with L as I. This can be reinforced by LQ, which now reads -T. Here only *at* and *it* fit the bill, but as we have G = A, again, L is left to represent I.

While tackling the two-letter groups consider GJ. This could be *am, an, as,* or *at.* The second and last we can forget, leaving us with either *am* or *as.* But which? Consider JU; if J is M, this would make JU equal MO, but if J is S we have AS and SO. There seems to be little doubt that J is S.

CUUV reads -OON. Again, with only the one letter missing, filling the gap should not prove too difficult. Our choice centres around the words, *boon, coon, goon, loon, moon* and *soon.* Not *noon,* for that would give us a palindrome (reading the same backwards as it does forwards). Of the six possibles, *coon* is really an abbreviation for racoon, while *goon* and *loon* are more in the nature of slang. *Boon,* meaning bounteous, benign, is unlikely in modern usage. This leaves either *moon* or *soon.* We know that J is S, therefore C must be M. There is other evidence to suggest this. Consider NVNCM (ENE-); a little thought and it is clear that the word *enemy* is a likely candidate here. This not only confirms C as M but gives M as Y.

It may help at this point again to consolidate findings with the blank alphabet, now twelve spaces less blank.

A B C D E F G H I J K L M N O P Q R S T U V W X Y Z

H R M   A   S   I Y E   T   O N D

A close examination shows that there is no *pattern,* so it must now be fairly obvious that this cipher is based on *random selection.* However, as the *blank alphabet* also serves as a record of ciphers broken, it is worth while continuing with it.

Having dismissed the possibility of a *pattern,* we must continue to decipher each letter individually and read through our cryptogram in the hope of discerning further clues.

KN GBN AUZLVS QU WBUZ MUYB EUUW GVW

E ARE HO IN TO DRO YO R OOD AND

RPUQALVS UV JYVWGM VLSAQ FYQ LQ KLPP

OTHIN ONS NDAY NI HT   T IT I

FN G QBLRTM UZNBGQLUV GJ NVNCM
E A TRI Y O ERAT ION AS ENEMY

GRQLXLQM LV QAN GBNG AGJ LVRBNGJNW LV
A TI I TY IN THE AREA HAS IN REASE D IN

QAN ZGJQ KNNT QANBN JAUYPW FN VU C UUV
THE AST   EE THERE SHO D E NO MOON

QAGQ VLSAQ JU KGQRA UYQ EUB QAN ZPGVN
THAT NI HT SO AT H O T OR THE   ANE

LQ KLPP CGTN UVN UXNBANGW EPLSAQ GVW
IT I   MA E ONE O ERHEAD   I HT AND

WBUZ QABNN ZGBGRAYQNJ UV LQJ BNQYBV.
DRO   THREE   ARA H TES ON ITS RET RN.

From this point onwards, many readers may feel that they
could now continue solo, and probably could without too
much difficulty. Although many of the still undeciphered
groups provide no problem whatsoever, it is worthwhile
taking each one in turn to examine its make-up.

Start by examining the third and the ninth groups. We
should be particularly interested in the word ending IN —.
It does not require much imagination to realise that the
missing letter is most likely to be G, giving us S as G. We
have now deciphered thirteen letters, half the alphabet.

In the third group, now reading HO-ING, only one letter
is missing. The possibilities are limited to *hoeing*,
homing and *hoping*. The last is obviously the most likely
and therefore it seems fairly safe to read P for Z. It is always
advisable to check other words to confirm findings, and
confirmation can be found in the fifth group WBUZ
(DRO-). By trying each letter of the alphabet in turn, we
arrive at the only feasible choice, DROP. So Z is P.

The sixth and seventh groups are complete except for one
letter. Take the sixth, now reading YO-R. Employing the
principle of trying each letter of the alphabet in turn, we
find that YOUR is the only one that really fits. Y is U. In
the seventh, EUUW (-OOD), using the same principle, we
arrive at four possibilities: *food*, *good*, *hood* and *wood*.
However, we already know that A is H, ruling out *hood*,
and that S is G, ruling out *good*. That leaves us with two
possibles, *food* and *wood*. The forty second group
provides the answer: it reads -OR. If E is W, we have WOR,
whereas if E is F, we have FOR. We need look no further.

94

LVRBNGJNW has been deciphered partly to read, IN-RE-ASED. Try the alphabet out and arrive at INCREASED. R is C. UXNBANGW reads O-ERHEAD. Surely this if OVERHEAD, and X is V.

We can go only a little further with this present cryptogram. The first group was agreed earlier to be *be*, *he*, *me*, or *we*. Try each in the context of the phrase made up by the first three words: it can only be WE ARE HOPING, and therefore K is T. The same principle is applied to discover the missing letter in FN: F is B.

KLPP is worth a closer look. That double-letter ending must reveal something, for only certain letters are found doubled at the end of a four-letter word: EE — as in *free*, LL — as in *ball*, and SS — as in *loss*. Our choice is E, L, or S. However, all but L have already been found. P is L.

Now consolidate again

```
A B C D E F G H I J K L M N O P Q R S T U V W X Y Z
H R M   F B A     S W I Y E   L T C G   O N D V U P
```

The cryptogram now reads

KN GBN AUZLVS QU WBUZ MUYB EUUW
WE ARE HOPING TO DROP YOUR FOOD

GVW RPUQALVS UV JYVWGM VLSAQ FYQ
AND CLOTHING ON SUNDAY NIGHT BUT

LQ KLPP FN G QBLRTM UZNBGQLUV
IT WILL BE A TRIC Y OPERATION

GJ NVNCM GRQLXLQM LV QAN GBNG AGJ
AS ENEMY ACTIVITY IN THE AREA HAS

LVRBNGJNW LV QAN ZGJQ KNNT QANBN
INCREASED IN THE PAST WEE THERE

JAUYPW FN VU CUUV QAGQ VLSAQ JU
SHOULD BE NO MOON THAT NIGHT SO

KGQRA UYQ EUB QAN ZPGVN LQ KLPP
WATCH OUT FOR THE PLANE IT WILL

CGTN UVN UXNBANGW EPSLAQ GVW WBUZ
MA E ONE OVERHEAD FLIGHT AND DROP

QABNN ZGBGRAYQNJ UV LQJ BNQYBV.
THREE PARACHUTES ON ITS RETURN

The only five letters for which we have not found cipher substitutes are J, K, Q, X and Z. These also happen to be at the lower end of the *frequency-list*. The *letter-count* shows that this cryptogram uses no D, H, I or O. These could be the lowest four letters in the frequency-list, leaving only K. The letter-count shows that all letters but T have now been accounted for. A quick look at the only missing letters in the cryptogram — TRIC-Y, WEE- and MA-E — confirms that T is K.

So the cryptogram has been completely deciphered. There are, admittedly, still four gaps in the blank alphabet, but as we now know that those four gaps represent the four letters at the end of the frequency-list, this omission need hardly concern us. In any future cryptogram based on the same cipher, these four might only put in one or two appearances. One or two new words in the next cryptogram would present few problems.

The cryptogram broken, the revealed message reads

WE ARE HOPING TO DROP YOUR FOOD
AND CLOTHING ON SUNDAY BUT IT WILL
BE A TRICKY OPERATION AS ENEMY
ACTIVITY IN THE AREA HAS INCREASED
IN THE PAST WEEK THERE SHOULD BE
NO MOON THAT NIGHT SO WATCH OUT
FOR THE PLANE IT WILL MAKE ONE
OVERHEAD FLIGHT AND DROP THREE
PARACHUTES ON ITS RETURN

This cryptogram was a simple one designed to bring out the basic principles involved in decipherment. In almost every case, letters fell into place after only a little thought. This will not always be the case. Many cryptograms will call for much more thought and imagination and many errors will be committed before the correct solution is found. Breaking ciphers is rather like tackling jigsaw puzzles and crossword puzzles — each piece is found only after thought and experiment. Above all, the cryptanalyst must be prepared to accept that errors will be made. Patience then comes into its own when perhaps hours of work have to be discarded and the whole process started again.

The following short secret message shows how a cryptogram can require several efforts before the correct solution is discovered.

ARIRE ORYVRIR GUNG LBHE SVEFG GEL

ZHFG OR GUR PBEERPG FBYHGVBA

As before, the first step is a *letter-count*

A	2	H	3	O	2	V	3
B	4	I	2	P	2	W	0
C	0	J	0	Q	0	X	0
D	0	K	0	R	8	Y	2
E	6	L	2	S	1	Z	0
F	3	M	0	T	0		
G	8	N	2	U	2		

There is a problem at the outset, for there are eight Gs and the same number of Rs. As these are the most frequent letters in use in the cryptogram, it is fairly safe to assume that one or the other represents the letter E. But which? Working in alphabetical order, try G as E.

ARIRE ORYVRIR GUNG LBHE SVEFG GEL
              E E   E E

ZHFG OR GUR PBEERPG FBYHGVBA
     E   E   E   E

At this point our next clues appear to be with the two three-lettered words, GEL and GUR. Three-letter words beginning with E are not over-common. *The Concise Oxford Dictionary* lists a mere twenty-three words of three letters which commence with E, excluding prefixes and suffixes: *ear, eat, eau, ebb, eel, e'en, e'er, eft, egg, ego, eke, elf, elk, ell, elm, emu, end, ens, eon, era, ere, eve* and *eye*. Many of these can be discarded as they do not seem to comply with the word pattern: *ebb, eel, e'en, e'er, egg, eke, ell, ere, eve* and *eye*. This leaves *ear, eat, eau, eft, ego, elf, elk, elm, emu, end, ens, eon* and *era*. This list can be further reduced by the exclusion of *eau* and *ens*, both rather rare, and *eon*, which is usually spelt *aeon*, and *eft* which is also rarely used today. We now have a shortlist of nine possibles, of which two refer to animals, one to a tree and one to a mythical fairy-like creature. These we can ignore for the time being. Our final list consists of *ear, eat, ego, end,* and *era.*

The letter-count shows that there are eight Rs. If G is to be E, we can assume that the R is T, second in the frequency-list. Our cryptogram now reads

ARIRE ORYVRIR GUNG LBHE SVEFG GEL
TT   T TTE   E   E E

ZHFG OR GUR PBEERPG FBYHGVBA
E TE T   TE   E

If we now look at GUR, it seems that the U must be A, to make the word EAT. And so through the cryptogram, changing U to A

ARIRE ORYVRIR GUNG LBHE SVEFG GEL
TT   T TTEA T   E E

ZHFG OR GUR PBEERPG FBYHGVBA
E T EAT   TE   E

We could go further, but, it should be increasingly clear that our whole attack set off on the wrong foot.

The logical move at this point is to return to square one and try R as E.

ARIRE ORYVRIR GUNG LBHE SVEFG GEL
EE   E EE

ZHFG OR GUR PBEERPG FBYHGVBA
E   E   E

Here we have two clues. OR can only be one of the following: *be, he, me* or *we.* GUR could be THE, the most common three-lettered word in usage and the E on the end increases its chances. Now try R as E, G as T (in the letter-count T also appears eight times and it is also the second letter in the frequency-list) and U as H

ARIRE ORYVRIR GUNG LBHE SVEFG GEL
EE   E EE TH T   T T

ZHFG OR GUR PBEERPG FBYHGVBA
T E THE   E T   T

This seems better. GUNG now reads TH-T and it takes little thought to see THAT, giving N as A

ARIRE ORYVRIR GUNG LBHE SVEFG GEL
E E E EE THAT   T T

ZHFG OR GUR PBEERPG FBYHGVBA.
T E THE   E T   T

Now return to OR and try each of the four possibilities in the context of THE: *be the? he the? me the? we the?* Although in certain cases the last could make sense, the most obvious is the first, giving O as B

```
ARIRE ORYVRIR GUNG LBHE SVEFG GEL
 E E  BE   E E THAT            T T


ZHFG OR GUR PBEERPG FBYHGVBA
   T BE THE     E T     T O
```

We have two further clues, one easier to see than the other. Taking the easier first, see the last group in the cryptogram and particularly its last four letters — T-O-. The cryptanalyst knows that in such a case the most common ending would be *tion*. Accepting this we now add V as I and A as N

```
ARIRE ORYVRIR GUNG LBHE SVEFG GEL
NE E  BE  I E E THAT          I  T T


ZHFG OR GUR PBEERPG FBYHGVBA.
   T BE THE O  E T O   TION
```

The second word of the cryptogram should now be fairly obvious, but before going further, let us not forget the blank alphabet, which may show some kind of pattern

```
A B C D E F G H I J K L M N O P Q R S T U V W X Y Z
N         T               B       E         I
```

Is there a pattern? At first glance it may well appear as if no pattern exists at the moment. Take a closer look. N is represented by A, while T is represented by G. Starting at N, say the alphabet — *n,o,p,q,r,s* — and come to T in its alphabetical order. Try the same from B — beneath O — and a pattern becomes clear.

```
A B C D E F G H I J K L M N O P Q R S T U V W X Y Z
N o p q r s T u v w x y z a B c d E f g h I j k l m
```

To verify this discovery simply try it out in the cryptogram

```
ARIRE ORYVRIR GUNG LBHE SVEFG GEL
NEVER BELIEVE THAT YOUR FIRST TRY


ZHFG OR GUR PBEERPG FBYHGVBA
MUST BE THE CORRECT SOLUTION
```

4

To a certain extent, the two disciplines that make up cryptology are eternally opposed to each other in a never-ending struggle to gain the upper hand. The cryptographer who puts messages into codes and ciphers must keep abreast of new developments in cryptanalysis and strive to devise a system which is beyond the latest techniques in the opposing study. The cryptanalyst who attempts to break codes and ciphers strives to keep abreast of new developments in cryptography and to find better ways of breaking cryptograms.

Here we will look briefly at some of the more complex ideas which this struggle has caused to develop in both areas of cryptology.

The cryptographer

In the first part of this book we considered various systems used to encode or encipher messages. Each system was studied on a basic and simple level. In almost every message, each word kept its original form. Take the following example

NTRAGF GB OR ERPNYYRQ NF FBBA NF CBFFVOYR

If nothing else, on intercepting this kind of cryptogram, the cryptanalyst can immediately see that it contains eight *words*: four two-letter, one four-letter, one six-letter and two eight-letter. Other clues are also quite clear. The BB in FBBA can only EE or OO. The first letter of that same word, F, also appears at the end of a two-letter word. This of course reduces its possibilities and with a little experimentation it can be deciphered. From the outset, then, this message *helps* rather than hinders the cryptanalyst.

The cryptographer accepts the possibility that his cryptogram may be intercepted and therefore endeavours to encipher the message in such a way as to make things as difficult as possible for anyone who attempts to read the message. One way is to disguise the *form* of the words.

Five-letter groups and transposition
We have already seen, when dealing with *transposition ciphers*, a few basic and very simple ideas for disguising words by dividing them into groups. Take the previous message

NTRAGF GB OR ERPNYYRQ NF FBBA NF CBFFVOYR

AGENTS TO BE RECALLED AS SOON AS POSSIBLE

To transmit the message in this, its original form, would, as we have seen, only help the cryptanalyst, therefore we disguise it. Nowadays, the most popular method is five-letter grouping.

AGENT STOBE RECAL LEDAS SOONA SPOSS IBLEX

NTRAG FGBOR ERPNY YRQNF FBBAN FCBFF VOYRX

Simply grouping the original message into groups of five letters gives a fairly effective *transposition cipher*. If this is combined with a *substitution cipher* it becomes a nightmare for the cryptanalyst. (The X at the end of the message is a *null*, and its purpose is to make up the last group of five: four *nulls* would be the most ever used in five-letter groups.)

Columnar transposition
Columnar transposition is even more effective. In this system, as its name suggests, messages are arranged in columns

```
A G E N T S
T O B E R E
C A L L E D
A S S O O N
A S P O S S
I B L E
```

The message is sent by writing out the first column, then the second, and so on

ATCAAI GOASSB EBLSPL NELOOE TREOS SEDNS

This gives six-letter groups and nulls can be added to the last two groups to make them up to six letters.

Keywords
A variation is the use of a *keyword*. Take the keyword

CIPHER. Each letter is numbered, from one to six, according to its order in the alphabet.

```
C   I   P   H   E   R
1   4   5   3   2   6
```

The message might then be written beneath this in similar fashion to the previous system

```
C   I   P   H   E   R
1   4   5   3   2   6

A   G   E   N   T   S
T   O   B   E   R   E
C   A   L   L   E   D
A   S   S   O   O   N
A   S   P   O   S   S
I   B   L   E
```

In writing out the message, the column beneath 1 is taken first, then the column beneath 2, and so on

ATCAAI TREOS NELOOE GOASSB EBLSPL SEDNS

In both cases, to decipher the message, the process is simply reversed, assuming in the latter case that the keyword is known.

Columnar transposition is equally effective using diagonal columns. Remaining with our message

```
A   G   E   N   T   S
T   O   B   E   R   E
C   A   L   L   E   D
A   S   S   O   O   N
A   S   P   O   S   S
I   B   L   E
```

Which of the diagonal columns is used first and in which order the diagonals are used depends entirely on choice. Obviously, both sender and receiver must know the sequence employed. In our diagonal, the first column will be A to S; the second, G to S; the third, E to N. Of course, with each column the number of letters decreases till we have the solitary S (from agents). The next column is T to O (from to); followed by C to E (from called), and so on.

The final cryptogram appears as

AOLOS GBLOS EEEN NRD S TASO CSPE ASL AB I

At a first glance this may appear to be defeating the main purpose of disguising the make-up of individual words in a cryptogram. A closer look will show that the system adds confusion for the cryptanalyst. The solitary S *does not* represent either A or I. The same applies to all the other groups — NRD does not represent a three-letter word.

To decipher the message, the cryptanalyst has to know how many letters are in each horizonal column and in which order the diagonal columns were taken. With this knowledge, he would write out the first group diagonally

```
A
   O
      L
         O
            S
```

The second group, placing the first letter next to the A, he again writes out diagonally

```
A G
   O B
      L L
         O O
            S S
```

The procedure is repeated till six letters have been placed along the top row

```
A G E N T S
   O B E R E
      L L E D
         O O N
            S S
```

The first letter of the next group obviously goes immediately beneath the A of *agents*

```
A G E N T S
T O B E R E
   A L L E D
      S O O N
         O S S
```

The first letter of the next group goes beneath the T, and so on till the message is complete.

Substitution ciphers can be used to disguise the make-up of words in a cryptogram. At a very simple level we can use a substitution cipher and then *transpose* the end result, a reversal of the first cipher in this section, although the product is identical.

To complicate matters, many cryptographers use a *biliteral substitution cipher*, which employs a *matrix*. In *biliteral substitution* each letter of the message has a two-letter cipher equivalent.

```
    A  B  C  E  F

D   A  B  C  D  E

G   F  G  H  IJ K

H   L  M  N  O  P

I   Q  R  S  T  U

J   V  W  X  Y  Z
```

To encipher

ENEMY ADVANCING

Find the E in the matrix and read off the two letters, along the vertical column first, then the horizontal column, giving DF to represent E. This is repeated with each letter of the message, till we have

DF HC DF HB JE   DA DE JA DA HC DC GE HC GB

This can be further complicated by grouping into fives

DFHCD FHBJE DADEJ ADAHC DCGEH CGB

perhaps with nulls added to the last group.

The various systems we have looked at so far all help the cryptographer to break up the natural form of words in the original message and in the cryptogram. However, the cryptographer does have another serious problem. In the English language, this is the most frequently-used letter — E. And this is the normal starting point for the cryptanalyst. If the cryptographer can somehow disguise the use of the E he will enhance the chances of his cryptogram remaining unbroken. There are a number of systems that have been devised to do just that.

One such system which is known as *digraphic substitution,* uses *digraphs,* or pairs of letters. It is not to be confused with *biliteral substitution,* which gives each plain letter a two-letter cipher equivalent. In *digraphic substitution,* the cryptographer takes two letters from the plain message and substitutes these with two cipher letters.

This involves the use of a *matrix,* but unlike the simple one-square matrix used with *biliteral substitution,* *digraphic substitution* uses a more complicated four-square *matrix.*

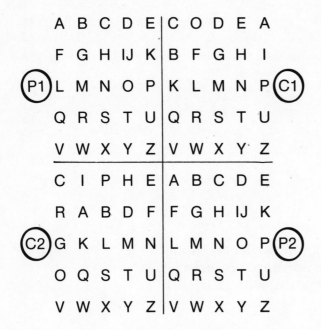

All four *matrices* are based on the 5 x 5 idea, which means that I and J are either doubled up or J is omitted altogether. Squares P1 and P2 are made up by simply writing out the alphabet. Squares C1 and C2, on the other hand, involve the use of a *keyword,* in this case, CIPHER and CODE. The keywords are written out first and gaps are filled by writing the alphabet out normallly except that whenever a letter that is already in the keyword is reached, one skips to the next letter.

Taking again

ENEMY ATTACKING

group the letters of the message into pairs

EN EM YA TT AC KI NG

106

The procedure for enciphering the message looks and sounds complicated, but it is quite simple once the basic fundamentals have been grasped.

Take the first pair of letters, EN, and locate them on a diagonal line, E in P1 and N in P2. The cipher equivalents appear at the opposite corners. The diagrams take the first four pairs.

```
        A  B  C  D (E) C  O (D) E  A
        F  G  H  IJ K| B  F  G  H  I
  (P1)  L  M  N  O  P| K  L  M  N  P (C1)
        Q  R  S  T  U| Q  R  S  T  U
        V  W  X  Y  Z| V  W  X  Y  Z
       ------------------------------
        C  I  P  H  E| A  B  C  D  E
        R  A  B  D  F| F  G  H  IJ K
  (C2)  G  K  L  M (N) L  M (N) O  P (P2)
        O  Q  S  T  U| Q  R  S  T  U
        V  W  X  Y  Z| V  W  X  Y  Z
```

Diagonal to E, we arrive at the other half of the pair, N. From N a vertical line finds D, along from E. Down vertically from E, we come to N, along from the first N. This gives DN as the cipher equivalent of the pair EN.

```
    A  B  C  D (E) C  O (D) E  A
    F  G  H  IJ K| B  F  G  H  I
    L  M  N  O (P) K  L (M) N  P
    Q  R  S  T  U| Q  R  S  T  U
    V  W  X  Y  Z| V  W  X  Y  Z
   ------------------------------
    C  I  P  H  E| A  B  C  D  E
    R  A  B  D  F| F  G  H  IJ K
    G  K  L  M  N| L  M  N  O  P
    O  Q  S  T  U| Q  R  S  T  U
    V  W  X  Y  Z| V  W  X  Y  Z
```

The second matrix gives DP as the cipher equivalent of EM.

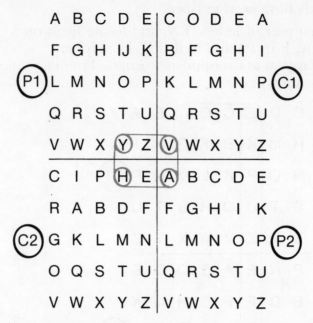

The next gives VH as the cipher equivalents for YA. The last example

gives TT as the cipher equivalent of TT. The procedure is repeated till every pair has been dealt with, giving the end result

DN DP VH TT PD AF FT

EN EM YA TT AC KI NG

Blaise de Vigenere, the inventor of the Vigenere table.

ET. ERVNT.
VT. CCMBLACEANT.
VERBA. ELOQVII. MEI.
Psalm. 18.

Tho. de leu f

Vigenere and polyalphabetic substitution

Even more complicated than *digraphic substitution* in concealing the frequency of letter-usage in any given cryptogram, is the *polyalphabetic substitution* system. As its name suggests, this system employs more than one alphabet in encipherment. Of the many variations, perhaps the best known is the Vigenere Table, named after Blaise de Vigenere, a Frenchmen of the 1500s who first introduced it.

```
  A B C D E F G H I J K L M N O P Q R S T U V W X Y Z

A A B C D E F G H I J K L M N O P Q R S T U V W X Y Z
A B C D E F G H I J K L M N O P Q R S T U V W X Y Z A
C C D E F G H I J K L M N O P Q R S T U V W X Y Z A B
D D E F G H I J K L M N O P Q R S T U V W X Y Z A B C
E E F G H I J K L M N O P Q R S T U V W X Y Z A B C D
F F G H I J K L M N O P Q R S T U V W X Y Z A B C D E
G G H I J K L M N O P Q R S T U V W X Y Z A B C D E F
H H I J K L M N O P Q R S T U V W X Y Z A B C D E F G
I I J K L M N O P Q R S T U V W X Y Z A B C D E F G H
J J K L M N O P Q R S T U V W X Y Z A B C D E F G H I
K K L M N O P Q R S T U V W X Y Z A B C D E F G H I J
L L M N O P Q R S T U V W X Y Z A B C D E F G H I J K
M M N O P Q R S T U V W X Y Z A B C D E F G H I J K L
N N O P Q R S T U V W X Y Z A B C D E F G H I J K L M
O O P Q R S T U V W X Y Z A B C D E F G H I J K L M N
P P Q R S T U V W X Y Z A B C D E F G H I J K L M N O
Q Q R S T U V W X Y Z A B C D E F G H I J K L M N O P
R R S T U V W X Y Z A B C D E F G H I J K L M N O P Q
S S T U V W X Y Z A B C D E F G H I J K L M N O P Q R
T T U V W X Y Z A B C D E F G H I J K L M N O P Q R S
U U V W X Y Z A B C D E F G H I J K L M N O P Q R S T
V V W X Y Z A B C D E F G H I J K L M N O P Q R S T U
W W X Y Z A B C D E F G H I J K L M N O P Q R S T U V
X X Y Z A B C D E F G H I J K L M N O P Q R S T U V W
Y Y Z A B C D E F G H I J K L M N O P Q R S T U V W X
Z Z A B C D E F G H I J K L M N O P Q R S T U V W X Y
```

The alphabet along the *top* represents the *plain* letters; those down the *side* represent the letters found in *keywords*; and the alphabets *within the square* represent the *cipher letters*.

Taking our old message

AGENTS TO BE RECALLED AS SOON AS POSSIBLE

the cryptographer must first devise a *keyword*. Let us use the word FAMILY. Grouping into fives, write out the message accordingly. Above the message write, repeatedly, the *keyword*

```
FAMIL   YFAMI   LYFAM   ILYFA
AGENT   STOBE   RECAL   LEDAS

MILFA   MILYF   AMILY
SOONA   SPOSS   IBLEX
```

To encipher the message, take the first letter of the message, A, and locate it along the top alphabet. Next, follow the A column *down* and arrive opposite the first letter of the keyword, F. The cipher letter is the letter which lies at the point where the corresponding columns intersect.

```
       ↓
  A    A B C D E F

  B │  B C D E F G
  C │  C D E F G H
  D │  D E F G H I
  E │  E F G H I J
→ F │  F G H I J K
  H │  H I J K L M
```

This gives F as the cipher equivalent of A. Repeat the procedure for the next letter of the message, G. Locate it along the top alphabet, follow the column down till it intersects the row of the second letter of the keyword, A, then read off the letter at the intersection

```
                 ↓
    A B C D E F G H

→ A A B C D E F G H

  B B C D E F G H I
```

which gives G as its own cipher equivalent. Repeat for the third letter

	A	B	C	D	E	F
A	A	B	C	D	E	F
B	B	C	D	E	F	G
C	C	D	E	F	G	H
D	D	E	F	G	H	I
E	E	F	G	H	I	J
F	F	G	H	I	J	K
G	G	H	I	J	K	L
H	H	I	J	K	L	M
I	I	J	K	L	M	N
J	J	K	L	M	N	O
K	K	L	M	N	O	P
L	L	M	N	O	P	Q
→M	M	N	O	P	Q	R
N	N	O	P	Q	R	S

giving Q as the cipher equivalent of E — this time. To prove the point, move to BE, with the second E. Use the same procedure of locating the E along the top alphabet, following down the column till the key letter above this E, is reached.

	A	B	C	D	E	F
A	A	B	C	D	E	F
B	B	C	D	E	F	G
C	C	D	E	F	G	H
D	D	E	F	G	H	I
E	E	F	G	H	I	J
F	F	G	H	I	J	K
G	G	H	I	J	K	L
H	H	I	J	K	L	M
I	I	J	K	L	M	N

This time M is the cipher equivalent of E.

The process continues with each letter of the message to give the final product

Keyword	FAMIL	YFAMI	LYFAM	ILYFA	MILYF	AMILY	FAMIL
Message	AGENT	STOBE	RECAL	LEDAS	SOONA	SPOSS	IBLEX
Cipher	FGQVE	QYONM	CCHAX	TPBFS	EWZLF	SBWDQ	NBXMX

A letter-count shows that there is very little difference between the number of times each letter appears.

A	1	H	1	O	1	V	1
B	3	I	0	P	1	W	2
C	2	J	0	Q	3	X	3
D	1	K	0	R	0	Y	1
E	2	L	1	S	2	Z	1
F	3	M	2	T	1		
G	1	N	2	U	0		

Which letter represents E?

This has effectively concealed the frequency of the E and the rearrangement of words into five-letter groups disguises the natural form of the whole word. Together they make up a cipher which is extremely difficult to break, even if one knows that the Vigenere Table has been employed.

To decipher the cryptogram is a relatively easy operation if one possesses the keyword. It is written above the letters of the cryptogram, in much the same way as it was placed above the letters of the message.

```
F A M I L    Y F A M I    L Y F A M    I L Y F A
F G Q V E    Q Y O N M    C C H A X    T P B F S

M I L Y F    A M I L Y    F A M I L
E W Z L F    S B W D Q    N B X M X
```

Take the last group of the cryptogram, NBXMX. To decipher this, take the first letter, N and find the diagonal column of Ns. Follow this column to the keyletter for N, along the vertical alphabet. N is deciphered by reading off the letter along the top alphabet.

For the second letter of the last word of the cryptogram, locate the keyletter above it, which in this case happens to be A. Now find the diagonal column of Bs and follow it to the point opposite the *keyletter* on the vertical alphabet.

The third letter, X, is tackled in exactly the same manner. Find the diagonal X column and follow it till its *keyletter* equivalent appears along the vertical alphabet. The letter appearing in the top alphabet is the plain letter of the message. Following the diagonal X column to M in the vertical alphabet, gives L in the top alphabet.

A B C D E F G H I J K L M N O P Q R S T U V W X

A	A B C D E F G H I J K . M N O P Q R S T U V W X
B	B C D E F G H I J K L . N O P Q R S T U V W X
C	C D E F G H I J K L M . O P Q R S T U V W X
D	D E F G H I J K L M N . P Q R S T U V W X
E	E F G H I J K L M N O . Q R S T U V W X
F	F G H I J K L M N O P . R S T U V W X
G	G H I J K L M N O P Q . S T U V W X
H	H I J K L M N O P Q R . T U V W X
I	I J K L M N O P Q R S . U V W X
J	J K L M N O P Q R S T . V W X
K	K L M N O P Q R S T U . W X
L	L M N O P Q R S T U V . X

M ←. . . . . X ← level with *keyletter*

The fourth letter is M with I
(from keyword FAMILY) as its
keyletter following a similar
procedure

N	N O P Q R S T U V W X ↑
O	O P Q R S T U V W X
P	P Q R S T U V W X
Q	Q R S T U V W X
R	R S T U V W X
S	S T U V W X
T	T U V W X
U	U V W X
V	V W X
W	W W X
X	X

A A B C D E F G H I J K L M

A	A B C D . F G H I J K L M
B	B C D E . G H I J K L M
C	C D E F . H I J K L M
D	D E F G . I J K L M
E	E F G H . J K L M
F	F G H I . K L M
G	G H I J . L M
H	H I J K . M

I ←. . . . M ← level with *keyletter*

J	J K L M ↑
K	K L M
L	L M
M	M

The last letter again shows just how effective the Vigenere
Table can be. Here there is another X to decipher, but
where as the first X had M as its keyletter, this time the X
has L as its keyletter.

A B C D E F G H I J K L M N O P Q R S T U V W X ↘

A	A B C D E F G H I J K L . N O P Q R S T U V W X
B	B C D E F G H I J K L M . O P Q R S T U V W X
C	C D E F G H I J K L M N . P Q R S T U V W X
D	D E F G H I J K L M N O . Q R S T U V W X
E	E F G H I J K L M N O P . R S T U V W X
F	F G H I J K L M N O P Q . S T U V W X
G	G H I J K L M N O P Q R . T U V W X
H	H I J K L M N O P Q R S . U V W X
I	I J K L M N O P Q R S T . V W X
J	J K L M N O P Q R S T U . W X
K	K L M N O P Q R S T U V . X
L	← . . . . X ← level with *keyletter*
M	M N O P Q R S T U V W X ↑
N	N O P Q R S T U V W X
O	O P Q R S T U V W X
P	P Q R S T U V W X
Q	Q R S T U V W X
R	R S T U V W X
S	S T U V W X
T	T U V W X
U	U V W X
V	V W X
W	W X
X	X

Here the M does not in fact fit in with the word deciphered so far and therefore, especially as it is the last letter, we can assume that this is a *null*, added to make up the last group of five.

The Cryptanalyst

While the cryptographer is doing his best to devise new, more secure, ciphers, the cryptanalyst is improving his knowledge in the fields of cryptography and cryptanalysis. He must keep up with all new developments in cryptography, especially in cipher machines. In his own field, he must constantly consolidate by practice.

Frequency lists

A cryptanalyst studies words. More precisely, he studies certain word patterns which are likely to occur in cryptograms. At a very basic level, he must know the frequency-list by memory. He needs to know it so well that to quote it would be no more difficult than quoting his own name and address.

First letter

The frequency-list is only one such familiar item. The cryptanalyst also knows the following list

T A O M H W B C D S F R H I Y E G L N P U J K Q Z

This is also a *frequency-list*, but of what? This list shows the frequency of the *first letter* in a given number of words. For although E is used more frequently than any other letter, T *starts* more words than any other letter.

Second letter

Which is the *most common second letter* in any given number of words? There is a frequency-list to show even this; the first nine being

H O E I A U N R T

Third letter

Again, there is a frequency-list to show *the most common third letter*. The first six are

E S A R N I

And the *last* letter? The first eighteen are

E T D S N R Y F L O G H A K M P U W

Eight letters are omitted from this particular frequency-list. In alphabetical order, they are B, C, I, J, Q, V, X, and Z. Of these, Q comes at the very bottom, for no English word ends with this letter. J comes second-last, with only one word to its name — *raj*. The others are also fairly obvious — only a rare word ends with any of those letters.

The order of the letters, always in descending order, is taken from the *average count* over thousands of words. *Never assume that the order will hold true for every passage.* Even the first letter in the lists may change places with some other letter. The secret is not to consider the letters individually but rather to look at groups. Three groups is usually sufficient: the first few letters are looked upon as the *high frequency group* (such as the six letters given for the third letter list); the next few are the *middle-frequency group* and the last few (as the eight letters omitted from the last letter list) are the *low-frequency group*. Within these three groups, the letters can and do change position. It is rare for a *low-frequency* letter to show a high frequency of use.

Nevertheless, these frequency-lists all concern individual letters only. The cryptanalyst must know these backwards, but his knowledge goes even further. In the English language, certain letters favour certain other letters as immediate companions.

Two-letter words

Two-letter words are few and far between. Most adults, and older children, could write out a complete list after only little thought. Although something such as the *Concise Oxford Dictionary* does list two-letter words wich most people never come across, the two-letter words in common usage number a mere twenty-four (twenty-five if one includes the word *ox*). Few readers should have any problem in finding these from their general knowledge of the language. The list appears in no particular order

am	be	do	to	it	we
an	by	is	me	as	in
my	up	so	on	no	us
he	if	or	go	of	at

On and *no* are unusual in that they are reversals of each other. We can go further with these two-letter words. For example, the most common single letter appearing in two-letter words is O, which features in eight of them; five times as the first and three times as the second. A, E, I, N and S feature in four of the above words; E always as the last letter, while I is always the first. The other three appear in both positions.

The table shows the number of times each letter appears and also its spread over the two positions.

Letter	Total	First	Last
a	4	4	0
b	2	2	0
d	1	1	0
e	4	0	4
f	2	0	2
g	1	1	0
h	1	1	0
h	4	4	0
m	3	2	1
n	4	1	3
o	8	5	3
p	1	0	1
r	1	0	1
s	4	1	3
t	3	1	2
u	2	2	0
w	1	1	0
	48	26	22

We can develop this idea by considering the spread of vowels and consonants. Of the twenty six letters which appear as the first letter, fifteen are vowels, while only eleven are consonants. The reverse situation is true of the twenty two letters which appear at the end of two-letter words. Only seven are vowels, while fifteen are consonants.

A frequency-list has also been produced to show which of these appears most often as a word

OF TO IN IT IS BE AS AT SO WE HE BY OR ON DO IF

Of perhaps even more importance to the cryptanalyst is the *digraph*, a combination of two letters which produce a particular sound. They are not to be confused with two-lettered words — a digraph does not form a *complete* word but merely a *part* of a word.

At a simple level, consider the double letters. Of the twenty-six letters in the English alphabet, only certain letters are found doubled in words and a knowledge of these is part of the cryptanalyst's armoury. Their frequency-list is:

LL EE SS DD TT FF RR NN PP CC MM GG

This in itself is sometimes enough, but it helps if one looks a little closer and appreciates that even double-letters have a pattern. SS, for example, appears at the end of a word more often than it does at the beginning. The reverse applies to RR.

Digraphs are not restricted to double letters. The following frequency-list shows the most common two-letter combinations which do not repeat a letter.

TH HE AN IN ER RE ES ON EA TI AT EN

Certain of these digraphs appear more frequently at the beginnings of words, while others appear more frequently at the ends of words. The most common digraph, TH, is, of course, and example of the former, being found in such common words as *the, that, then,* and *there.* The digraph ER, on the other hand, is usually found at the end: *other, better.*

Three-letter words

Along with a knowledge of digraphs, the cryptanalyst must know something of *trigraphs;* combinations of three letters.

The frequency-list below shows the most common three-letter words in use in the English language.

THE AND FOR WAS HIS NOT BUT YOU ARE HER HAD ALL

The last of these, ALL, is of particular interest, in that its pattern is distinctive. The number of three-letter words with a double ending is limited. A few are

ADD BEE EBB EGG FEE ILL LEE NEE ODD SEE TOO

In simple cryptology, perhaps secret messages being passed between two friends, these words can serve as vital clues. It goes without saying that, of these, ALL is the most common.

Other patterns appear in three-letter words. Take the *palindrome,* reading the same backwards as it does forwards. The number is limited and they tend to stand out even when enciphered

DAD EVE GAG MUM NUN PIP DUD SOS NON POP EYE

These should be borne in mind. In modern cryptograms with letters re-arranged into groups of five these would not be obvious at the start, but the pattern may begin to show later.

To return to trigraphs. As with digraphs, one has to consider which are more frequent at the beginnings of words and which are more common at the ends. With trigraphs this is easier to do, as can be seen from the frequency-list

THE AND THA ENT ION TIO FOR NDE HAS NCE

It is perhaps worth noting that the first two trigraphs are also the most common three-letter words in use. The importance of looking for and recognising the trigraph, THE, cannot be overstressed. One trigraph not listed above is ING. This combination is worth looking for at the end of words.

Four-letter words

Tetragraphs are combinations of four letters. Here we enter rather difficult territory, as many tetragraphs, or four-letter combinations which we suspect could be tetragraphs, may be no more than trigraphs with an S added to give the plural. Take the trigraph ENT. Assume that we have it in a cryptogram as AESD and that we suspect ENT to be part of this word ending. Is the D an S, or is the A an M (to give the tetragraph, MENT)? Or again, take the word ending, WRTY. We suspect that the trigraph ION is there, but is the Y an S or is the W a T, giving us TION (the most common tetragraph)?

Among four-letter words, certain word patterns are worth considering. Take these enciphered words

ONYY YBFF OHSS

What is immediately noticeable? The double-letter ending. The possibilities are limited. Consider these

QRRQ ABBA GBBG

Here the palindrome is obvious, and, as four-letter palindromes are not common, deciphering these words should not prove too difficult.

Of course, such simple clues only appear in simple cryptograms. However, the last frequency-list is worth studying, for it shows the most common four-letter words in use and even the most difficult cryptogram has to employ such words, albeit disguised. Note, too, the digraph, TH and the trigraph, THE.

THAT WITH HAVE THIS WILL YOUR FROM THEY KNOW

Anyone considering taking the study of cryptanalysis a little further would be well advised to search out a good dictionary for examples of all the word patterns covered in this book and to record any new examples in a *word pattern book*. Those words we have covered are elementary to the practised cryptanalyst, but even the experts use a *word pattern book*.

From recording digraphs and trigraphs which appear at one end or the other of words, the student might progress to observing rather more complex word patterns, such as those listed under the *ABA pattern*. Trigraphs which appear almost anywhere

ENE**MY** AGA**INST** EXE**RCISE**

and again

GALAXY PREDECESSOR STRATAGEM

From trigraphs of this nature, move on to consider words in the perhaps even more interesting ABBA class. These are tetragraphs and, again, appear in almost any position of a word. Simply collecting them from a dictionary is a fascinating pastime, but to the cryptanalyst they are almost indispensable.

ATTA**CK** AFF**AIR** OPPO**NENT**

OPPO**SITE** IMMI**GRATE** VESSEL

INTELLE**CT** CORRO**SIVE**

The point here, for those who have not already noticed, is that in every case the A of either ABA or ABBA class words is a vowel, while the B is always a consonant. This holds true even when we move on to the more complex ABACA class of words.

PREDECE**SSOR** ELEME**NTARY** INQU**ISITI**VE

V**IRIDITY** IRITIS APPEND**ICITIS**

Knowledge of these word patterns is an important part of the cryptanalyst's equipment. But knowing that ABA, ABBA or ABACA class of words exists is one thing, having the flair, the imagination, the stubborn patience to search for them in a cryptogram is something else. It is here that many amateur cryptanalysts fall down. They find the E and then seem to expect the remainder to open out before them as if overcoming the first hurdle ensured an easy time for the rest of the cryptogram. To repeat earlier advice, there are no magic wands in breaking a cipher, there is only hard work, using all the tools available. Word patterns are an essential item in the cryptanalyst's toolbag. *Knowing* what to look for is not enough, *one has to look for it!*

The reader is invited to put theory into practice on the following twelve cryptograms. Perhaps it would be advisable first to re-read the earlier section on the basic techniques of breaking a cipher, followed by another reading of the second part of this present section. Never forget that a knowledge of how cryptographers use ciphers may be of assistance. Above all, *look* and always be prepared to go back to square one.

All twelve messages are pure fiction. As far as possible they have been graded in degrees of difficulty; the first being relatively simple, in so far as it follows more or less the cipher tackled in an earlier section of this book. Each one increases a little in difficulty till the last, which is quite difficult.

Twelve secret messages

One   OCZ ADMNO XDKCZM DI OCDN GVNO NZXODJI
JA OCZ WJJF NCJPGY WZ V NDHKGZ JIZ
OJ WMZVF VN DO DIXGPYYZN IZVMGT VGG
OCZ XGPZN OCVO RZ AJGGJRZY DI OCZ
XCVKOZM JI XJYZ-WMZVFDIB. OCZMZ VMZ IJ
CVMY RJMYN VIY IJ XVOXCZN VOOVXCZY

Two   GF Q SOZZST ZIGXUIZ NGX VOSS LGGF
KTQSOLT ZIQZ ZIT LTEGFR EGRT LIGXSR
WT FG DGKT ROYYOEXSZ ZIQF ZIT SQLZ
GFT VQL TBTETHZ ZIQZ ZG DQAT DQZZTKL
Q SOZZST DQKRTK O IQCT OFESCRTR ZIT
YOKLZ-HTKLGF LOFUXSQK. GZITKVOLT QSS ZIT
ESXTL QKT OF OFESXROFU RGXWST DORRSTL
QFR EGDDGF TFROFUL

Three   WHVFDI HZZFVSB HR RWS RWFZB NXBS FD
RWS CSNRFXD EXP CWXPOB KS MXZS RWHD
YZSYHZSB RX RHNAOS FR GFRWXPR RWS
FDNOPCFXD XU RWS FDBSUFDFRS HZRFNOS
HDB RWS UFZCR YSZCXD CFDIPOHZ HC RWSE
HOGHEC MHAS MHRRSZC RWHR MPNW SHCFSZ
WXGSVSZ MHDE XRWSZ NOPSC WHVS KSSD
OSUR FD RX WSOY EXP XPR

Four   YS IFS VEY MEFS XTIV TIDB YIQ XTFEGKT
XTS ACNTSFO CV XTCO DIOX OSAXCEV IVJ
XTSFSBEFS QEG OTEGDJ RS NFSNIFSJ XE
IAASNX XTIX EV EAAIOCEVO XTS BFSWGSVAQ
DCOX JESO VEX TEDJ XFGS. EXTSF ADGSO
TIPS IDOE RSSV DSBX EGX

Five   WDTB TBR CDCTB NKAR MGG TWK GRTTRQRA
WKQAS MQR ORDJH GRCT KUT WBDNB YKU NMJ
NKJSDARQ ORDJH LQRLRQMTDKJ CKQ TBR GMST
NKAR WBRQR MGG TBR GRTTRQS BMVR ORRJ
MQQMJHRA DJTK HQKULS RMNB HQKUL NKJTMDJDJH
CDVR GRTTRQS MJA WDTB JUGGS MAARA
DJNQRMSDJH TBR ADCCDNUGT

Before beginning the following harder cryptograms,
transcribe them into five-letter groups.

Six   NAPEHMNTIS PBMOYUHLNAPFIMN SBUUBTQENB
GNAPOIIDHM HEENAPEPNNPLMHLPHLLHGRPSB
GNIRL IQJMI UUBVPBUYIQ FHGHRPNIOL PHNBA
BMIGPTIGMBSPLYI QLMPEJMIFP NABGRIUHGP
XJPLN BGNAPUBPESIUTLY JNHGHEYMBMNAPHQ
NAILA IJPMN AHNYI QAHVPPGCIY PSNABMMFHE
EHSVPGNQLPBGNINAPSHL DFYMNPLBPMIUPMJ
BIGHR PHGSGIWOBSMYIQHEEHEHMNUHLPWPEE

Seven   UAEHTWROHTLDLUDOTEKI ERPXE SIHSS KNAHT
LAOTSSOHTLOVNIE IDEVL TTUPNOCGNINASED
HPICD OTSREEHTEGIHOTR EFIWS ERROFGNIDA
IFEHT RPTSRNAFOOEROFDRUOCNEMEGAVIGTN
POTNEOFLUAHSIHR NIPLE IKROWTUOGNCEMOS
REHPI TDNASPEHTOSILBU FSREHKAMROTIGNI
ISSOP OFFELBAEHTRROHTUEESOTFESIH STROF
IRPNI ZYXTN

Eight   TAEMOEVBLUQHOYMTLSOCJWCQCRCBQGYQBJM
GETOCKQMLQBTBLKPBMAEOOEVEOQBKSTAELO
HEOLRECPASOLUMLRRBVEGETTEOTABQMOEQE
KTHOYMTLSOCJBQI CQEHLKCPBMAEOUQBKSTA
EFEYWLOHPBMAEOCKHLKPETABQFEYWLOHBQI
OLFEKTAEOEQTQALUGHIENUBTEQBJMGEZQQZ

124

Nine　CBAQKWSLBLBKEUAMQOTMLAHUMWAHQMWKGTL
CNLCFLCGTHBECNMHKGTHHBLKGWQKWSLBKHR
CSSMOBSSMQEBKHRJUTSMTFEUHAMMNKGTALB
FQMWAQBGQKFBKQRKAMEKGTIMT QBOKGTLMFQ
MWAQBGIMTMHBSKVHMVLCTCTKYKQCKGTMTAK
TLKSK QOSBWTBGWTURNLCGTYLBKKSMTSSMHB
TBKRAHUMWSQKGTMSOBGQKOKQKGWKKSMTYTC
HCRBSCGLMTSYHBLBTOYQEKGTI MSKCTCHBUP
KGTLMGEUJYQKVSALKOKASQKGOCENLCFBKQR

Ten　34 32 14 45 14　41 41 42 12 44　44 34 24 41 31
45 22 34 44 21　15 23 42 45 12　33 15 14 11 53
34 41 41 13 12　45 21 12 13 45　14 34 13 45 12
12 11 14 13 23　12 32 45 22 31　11 12 44 45 21
12 11 11 12 13　41 31 45 45 31　15 34 13 45 22
31 14 41 42 22　14 24 31 45 14　13 25 42 31 15
22 14 42 44 42　15 12 52 31 45　22 31 42 12 34
13 45 45 22 14　45 34 13 21 15　23 42 45 12 41
12 33 23 45 22　31 44 31 21 15　31 45 34 44 34
11 14 33 34 13　14 45 34 12 13　14 13 25 53 34
41 41 34 13 33　13 31 44 44 45　12 44 51 32 32
31 15 44 31 45

Eleven　AO II UO OE OUEO AA OO IU EIAI EI EO IE EI
AI EU AI EI EO EA OO IU AO AAIA AO AE IU EI
AI UO OE OU OAEO UO UE EI EEEE IA OE AU AA
AO IE EI AI UO OE OU AI AA EIEE II EI AA EU
EI AO AU IO EOAU EI EO AI EI UI AE EI AI OO
OO IU AO AA IAAO AE IU EI AI AO AA AE EO AI
OO AO IA OU EEEO AI IE AO II II AO IA OU EE
OO OO OE EU AIEI EO EA EU OUOO OO IU EI EE
EO AA OO UE AOEE EE EU EI OAOE AI EI IE AO

II II AO IA OU   EE OO EO AA AOOO OU AA EI AA
OO UE OE IA AOAE IU EI AI AA UO AA OO EI OA
AA OO OE AE AIOE IE OU IA EI OE AU EI IA AI
UO AE OO OE IOAI EO OA UU UI

Twelve   EE EE DE OA DE ER DA CB DA DK OE EK CR EE SA
DE DE SA EK CK DA CE ER CE DA EA EE CE ER ER
EK CE CK OA EK SA SR DA EE EA DB CK CB DK OE
DA CK DE CK SE CA EE OK OE CB EK DB EE DB SE
SA EE OA CK SB ER DB OA OB SE DA OB DE ER CK
DB CB CA CB SE EK EK OR EA DB CK DE CK DE SE
CR DB EA OE CK EE CA ER CK SE CK OA OE CK CB
EE DR SA SE SE

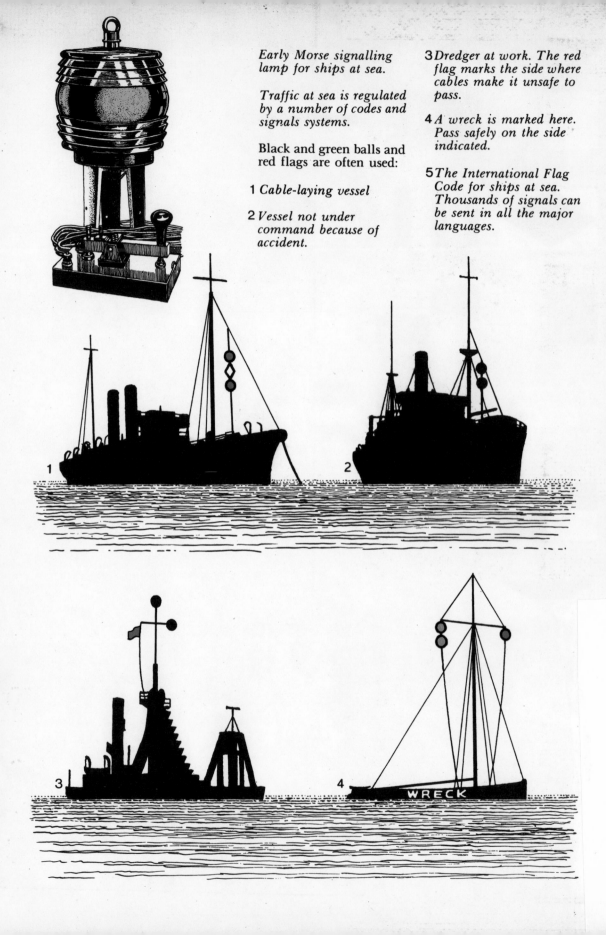

Early Morse signalling lamp for ships at sea.

Traffic at sea is regulated by a number of codes and signals systems.

Black and green balls and red flags are often used:

1 Cable-laying vessel

2 Vessel not under command because of accident.

3 Dredger at work. The red flag marks the side where cables make it unsafe to pass.

4 A wreck is marked here. Pass safely on the side indicated.

5 The International Flag Code for ships at sea. Thousands of signals can be sent in all the major languages.

WRECK